Presented to

Yasmin

from

Auntie Marie & Uncle Neil

Date _December 25, 1997_

Stories from the Bible

Stories from the Bible

Text by Sheri Dunham Haan
Illustrations by Samuel J. Butcher

BAKER BOOK HOUSE
Grand Rapids, Michigan 49506

This special paperback edition issued 1995 by
Baker Books
a division of Baker Book House Company
P.O. Box 6287, Grand Rapids, Michigan 49516-6287

ISBN: 0-8010-4085-X

Formerly published under the title
Good News for Children

Printed in the United States of America

To **God**
with thanksgiving
for
Chad Allen
Shelly Ann
and
Keith Michael

I have no greater joy than to hear
that my children walk in truth
(3 John 4).

Contents

3. The Good News   63

4. Acts of Hate   103

8. Acts of Disobedience   175

9. Deeds of Obedience   199

10. Acts of Pride   211

14. Jesus Is Coming Again! 267

16

Preface

Precious Moments Stories from the Bible (formerly titled *Good News for Children*) is my way of answering the many questions I have been asked by parents and teachers about Bible stories, books, and children. This book is different from others precisely because I have tried to write a book that will help you teach your children about God.

This book takes a thematic approach. The creation, fall, and salvation of man are treated in the first two chapters. Then the themes of obeying God or Satan are carried out in chapters which focus on concepts such as love, hate; obedience, disobedience; humility, pride. Stories which appeal to children and teach these lessons have specifically been chosen. The final chapter is concerned with living for Jesus until He comes again.

Vocabulary has been kept very simple. These Bible stories can easily be read to preschool children with the assurance that they will understand the main ideas of the stories.

The reading level is low enough that second- and third-graders can read this book without difficulty. The large print will make reading easier for them and encourage them to feel that this book has been written just for them.

Sam Butcher's unique art appeals to children. They love the big eyes, subtle humor, and readily identify with the joy or sadness the figures convey.

Precious Moments Stories from the Bible is written primarily for home use, but it is also the kind of book that Bible school leaders and Sunday school teachers will give to their students to help them learn about God and salvation. School teachers could use it as a springboard for teaching the Bible in thematic units. But most important, it helps young children understand Bible truths.

Sheri Dunham Haan

Stories from the Bible

1 God Makes the World

Nothing at All
(Genesis 1:2)

When you were playing today,
what did you see?
a furry kitten?
a busy ant?
Maybe you saw
children playing.

God Makes the World

If it was warm,
you might have
seen a fuzzy flower,
a beautiful butterfly,
or some buzzing bees.

Perhaps you
played outside.

If it was very cold you might have rolled in the snow and made angels. Maybe you went ice-skating. Isn't it fun to see, hear, and smell all the beautiful things God made for us?

Did you know that long, long ago there were no trees or flowers? No children played in the sunshine or in the snow. In fact, there was nothing at all. Everywhere it was empty and dark. God and His angels were the only living beings. They were living in heaven.

Maybe you wonder how the world got

God Makes the World

here. Just keep reading, and you'll find the story of God making His lovely world.

Day and Night

(Genesis 1:3–5)

On the first day God divided the day from the night.

God often walked through the darkness and emptiness. One day He had something very special in mind as He looked around Him. God decided to make the world.

You may think that this would be impossible to do because there was nothing for God to use. There was no lumber, bricks, or cement. Everywhere it was black and still. But you must remember that God can do all things. That is why it was not difficult for God. The only thing He said was, "Let there be light."

As soon as God spoke, the darkness began to move. Light began to show where darkness had been. The darkness and the light kept moving until they were separated. It was no longer black everywhere because God had made light.

God looked at what He had made and He liked it very much. God said that He would call the light, day. The darkness He called night. That was the first day.

Heaven and Earth

(Genesis 1:6–8)

The second day God made sky and earth.

On the second day God looked at what He had made the day before, the day and the night. He was happy with it. But today He had something else on His mind. He was going to make the earth and sky.

God spoke. He said that the sky should be over the earth. And from nowhere the sky began to move together and the earth came together. When it was finished, the sky was above the earth just like God wanted it to be. God said that He would call the sky, heaven. That was the end of the second day. Now there was day and night and heaven and earth. Again God was very pleased with what He had made—all of it out of nothing.

Land and Water

(Genesis 1:9–13)

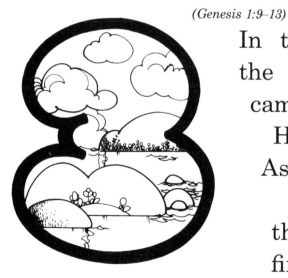

Dry land appeared on the third day.

In the morning of the third day God came to the world He was making. As He looked at it, He knew that He wasn't finished. There were so many things He wanted to make. But on this day He was going to make the land and the water.

Just as before, God spoke. This time He said that all the water should come together and stay by itself. The land should be by itself and it should be dry land.

As the land moved together God put green grass on it. He also put gardens and trees on the land. Some of the trees were tall and thin. Others were short and fat like bushes. God put blossoms and fruit on some of these trees. The world was beginning to look more like God wanted it to look.

Even the water was now alone. Some of it was put in very large places. These were the oceans and the seas. Some of the water ran in wide, deep streams and rivers. The tiny moving brooks came, too. You can almost hear the music that the waters were making. The waves of the large oceans slapped on the shores. The

little streams made high tinkling sounds as they trickled down the sides of the rocks.

God looked at the land and the water. His world looked more beautiful every day. The morning and the evening of the third day were over.

Skylights

(Genesis 1:14–19)

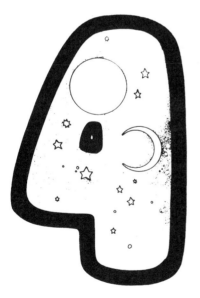

On the fourth day God made the sun, moon, and stars.

As God came to the world on the fourth day He knew just what He would do. He wanted to make lights for the sky. This is how we tell day from night and why we have days, weeks, and years. This is how we tell time.

God said that the sun should be the light of the day. Immediately the big, round, hot sun came into the sky and made the day look alive. The green of the plants was brighter. The sun made the quiet water look like a giant mirror. The sun warmed everything it could touch. It helped the gardens grow strong and green.

For the night God made another light. It is the moon. It's the bigger light that you see in the sky at night. It is the light you often look for if your bedroom seems too dark. There are other little lights in the sky. They are the stars that play hide-and-seek with you when you are in bed.

When God had finished this, the night of the fourth day came, and all was dark and still, but the stars were shining.

Perch and Peacocks

(Genesis 1:20–23)

The fish and birds appeared on the fifth day.

The world that God had made looked very beautiful. Trees and flowers sprouted and bloomed. There were glowing lights in the sky, and the waters were shades of blue and gray-green.

But in the air and water there was nothing living yet. So God spoke and soon the oceans and seas were filled with whales, porpoises, clams, and starfish. The lakes were full of perch, pike, bluegills, bass, crabs, and turtles. Trout began to swim in the streams.

God spoke to fill the air with colorful birds. Some of the birds were strong and flew many miles without stopping. Others could fly, but weren't so strong. They stayed closer to the earth and perched in the bushes and on the lower branches of the trees. God gave the birds feathery coats of rainbow colors.

You can imagine the wonderful sights God must have seen on the evening of this day. The sun began to tuck itself  behind the hills. The birds came to their perches to roost for the night. God looked at all these things He had made on the fifth day. He was glad He had made them.

Man and Animals

(Genesis 1:24–28)

As God walked about His world on the morning of the sixth day, He knew that

He would soon be finished. There were living things in the sea and in the air. But there was nothing living on the ground.

God looked over the world and said that animals should be made and that they should have babies. Then God made the animals of every size, shape, and color you can think of. Some were as tall as the giraffe and the dinosaur. They munched

leaves from the highest branches. The squirrels and the monkeys were smaller but quicker. They could turn and scamper away as they teased the zebras. God liked all the animals He had made.

Even after the animals had been made, God was not finished. There was no one to take care of the animals and the gardens.

God Makes the World

There was no one at all who could help them. So God said that He would make a man who would be very much like God Himself.

God took some of the dust from the ground. He worked with it until He had made the man exactly as He wanted him. But before man would be complete, God had to breathe a breath of air into him so he could live.

On the sixth day God made man.

Now the animals had a friend to care for them. Man was much different from everything else God had made. Man had a soul. That means that he could speak, think, and love. God and man often talked together. God told the man that it was his job to take care of this lovely world.

Finally the daylight began to dim. The moon peeked over the mountains. It climbed higher and higher until it joined the stars. The sixth day was over. God was pleased because everything He had made was very good.

God Rests

(Genesis 2:1–3)

On the seventh morning God came to His world but He did not work. He did not make anything at all. The Bible tells us that God rested on the seventh day. That is the very reason that we are supposed to rest and praise God on one day of the week.

God rested on the seventh day.

As God rested He must have listened to

the sounds of his world. The fish splashed water as they played in the lakes. The birds chirped and laughed as they watched

the animals below running through the grasses. Some of the animals napped, and God could hear the sounds of sleep. Even the humming of the song birds could be heard as God rested.

Now you know the story of God's world and how He made all of it out of nothing. When you see and hear the sights and sounds of God's world,

sing to Him and thank Him for all these good things He made.

God Makes the World

2 The World Becomes Sinful

A Lovely Home
(Genesis 2:8–9, 15–17)

God made a special place for Adam. It was called the Garden of Eden. There were so many beautiful plants and trees in it. God knew that it would be a pleasant place for Adam to live. There were rivers flowing through it and there were many precious stones. The Garden of Eden must have looked even lovelier than the most colorful and well-kept park you have ever seen. God brought Adam to this garden and told him that it would be his home. He should care for it and give names to every bird, plant, and animal.

Before God left, He had something very important to say. God told Adam about the many different trees He had made. Adam could see the fruit on some of these trees. It looked so ripe and juicy. God said that he could eat any fruit from these trees except from one. That was the Tree of Knowledge of Good and Evil. God explained to him that if he should ever eat even one piece of fruit from this tree, he would be sinning and would die. Eating from the tree would be sin because it would be disobeying God. After God finished speaking, He left Adam in the garden by himself.

A Wife for Adam

(Genesis 2:18, 21–25)

Taking care of God's new world would be a big task. Adam might need some help. There were many animals and birds, but they couldn't help Adam. They could not talk to him and keep him company. God didn't want Adam to feel lonely. So God made Adam fall sound asleep. Then God took one of Adam's ribs, one of the bones from his chest. From this bone, God made a woman and gave her a soul.

Adam and Eve must have talked together about all of the beauty around them. They enjoyed being together. They loved to sing and laugh. They explored their new home and played with all the animals. They were happy and peaceful in the lovely Garden of Eden.

God's Enemy

(Matthew 25:41)

Adam and Eve were busy in the garden. There was much to be done. They enjoyed being together and helping each other. The garden must have been a very warm place to live, because Adam and Eve didn't wear any clothes. They weren't embarrassed and ashamed because there was no sin. The world was pleasant and beautiful.

But there was something unlovely in God's world. That was Satan and his angel friends. Sometimes Satan is called the Devil. You may wonder how these sinful creatures got into God's world.

Before God made the world, He lived with His angels. All of God's angels served Him then, just like boys and girls of today should. But one of the angels God had made thought he could be as great and powerful as the One who made him. This can't be. It is a sin for anyone to think that he is as good or better than God. When this angel sinned, God had to send him away from heaven. This sinful angel was Satan, and he took other angel friends with him.

When God made the beautiful Garden of Eden, Satan came to visit it. He wanted others to sin and be like him. He thought and thought about how he would get Adam and Eve to disobey God.

A Wicked Trick
(Genesis 3:1–7)

At last Satan knew exactly what he would do to trick Adam and Eve. He would enter a snake and wait for a time when he could talk to one of them alone. It would be much easier to trick just one person, he thought.

One day he noticed the perfect moment. Eve was sitting by herself in the shade, waiting for the warm afternoon sun to go down. Suddenly she realized that she wasn't alone, because a voice asked, "Eve, did God tell you that you couldn't eat from all of the trees in the garden?"

"You're right," answered Eve. "We may eat from all of them except one. We may not eat from the Tree of Knowledge of Good and Evil. That's the tree right over there. It's in the middle of the garden." Eve pointed to it. Then she added, "God said that Adam and I would die if we ever eat any of the fruit from that tree."

Satan smiled. "So that's what God said. Oh, Eve! You won't die if you eat from it. In fact, if you do, you will be like God. You will know good from evil." Then Satan waited.

Eve glanced quickly at the tree. She walked over to it. She noticed how large and ripe the fruit was. How tasty it looked! While she stood there she thought to herself, "If I eat this fruit I'll be wise."

Then she forgot what God had said. She picked one of the nicest pieces and began to eat. She did exactly what God had told her not to do. She called to Adam and he ate some of it too. Both of them, Adam and Eve, ate from the tree which God had forbidden.

Satan was so very pleased. His wicked trick worked. Both Adam and Eve sinned.

Leaving Home

(Genesis 3:8–17, 23–24)

God knew what had happened to His world. He knew that Adam and Eve had disobeyed Him. So he looked for them in the garden. He called out, "Adam, Eve, where are you?"

Adam answered, "We're hiding. We are so ashamed because we disobeyed You. And we are naked. We tried to put some fig leaves together to cover ourselves." Adam and Eve crouched down behind the bushes. Then Adam added, "We're afraid."

God said, "Adam, how do you know you are naked? Why are you and Eve so embarrassed? Did you eat from the Tree of Knowledge of Good and Evil?"

Adam quickly said, "Well, it was really Eve's fault. She gave me a piece of the fruit, so I did take some."

Then God called to Eve, "What have you done? Did you eat the fruit from the tree?

Eve was ashamed because she knew that she had sinned. Her face turned red and she felt hot. But she knew that she had to answer God's question. She said, "It was really Satan's fault. He tricked me. He told me that I would be very wise if I ate, so I did take a piece."

Then God turned to the snake and said, "Because you did this, you will have to crawl around on your belly for the rest of your life. You will eat the dust from the ground."

Adam and Eve were frightened as they listened. Then God looked at Eve and said, "Because you have sinned, Eve, you will have pain when you have children. And your husband will rule over you." And to Adam He said, "You will have to work very hard. When it is hot you will sweat and your back will get tired. You will have to work this hard to make a living and have enough to eat, and some day you will die."

Before God left them, He made clothes

out of animal skins so Adam and Eve would have something to wear. What a sad day this was! Now God's peaceful and lovely world was covered with sin. God made Adam and Eve leave the beautiful Garden of Eden. To make sure that they didn't come back, He put angels and a flaming sword to guard the gate.

Hard Work

(Genesis 4:1–2)

Now the world was very different from when God created it. Adam and Eve worked so hard. Things were just like God said they would be. Adam planted a garden and he had to work to make it grow. Eve had to cook the food. She didn't have shiny pots and pans. She had no cans of food she could open, and she didn't have a dishwasher. Living was hard work.

The animals were different too. They chased and pounced to kill each other for food. Birds pecked and clawed. Eagles swooped to get their supper.

Before sin, Adam could tumble and play with the largest of all lions. But now he had to be very careful. A hungry lion or bear could kill him in a moment.

Diseases killed some of the plants and grasses. Or if the sun was too hot it would scorch the leaves. The burned plants would turn yellow and brown and then die. Sometimes insects ate the plants.

At times Adam and Eve got sick. Their stomachs ached or their feet were sore. If they felt too badly, they had to rest for a few days, like you do when you are ill.

Later two boys were born to Adam and Eve. Sometimes they played together and had fun. But other times they kicked and hollered and fought.

Yes, sin was in the world and it is still here today. God says, "For all have sinned and come short of the glory of God" (Romans 3:23).

The World Becomes Sinful

God Punishes Sin

(Romans 3:23; Genesis 32-33)

The Bible tells us that God will punish us for our sins. We all sin. You do. I do. Our punishment will be living far away from God and His love. That would be like leaving your home and never ever being able to come back.

Something like this happened to Jacob once. He did a very bad thing. He tricked his blind old father and stole his brother's blessing. His brother Esau was so angry that he said he'd kill Jacob. Jacob was afraid. So he had to run away. He packed a few clothes and left. He had to leave his father's house. He had to go far, far away from his parents' love.

Many years later, Jacob missed his brother. But he didn't know if Esau still hated him. So he sent this message.

Dear Esau,

I would like to see you again. Since I left home, I have become rich. I own a lot of cattle. I hope you will see me.

Jacob

When the messengers came back, they had bad news. "Esau is coming to see you. He has an army with him. Four hundred men!"

Jacob was scared stiff! What would he do? His sin had caused an awful mess. When he could think straight, he figured out a plan. He divided every-thing he owned into two groups. If Esau killed

one group of cattle, the other one could get away.

Jacob prayed to God for safety.

Then Jacob gathered a present for Esau. It was quite a gift! He sent it ahead to Esau:

200 nanny goats
20 billy goats
220 sheep
30 camels and their calves
40 cows
10 bulls
30 donkeys

That night Jacob tried to sleep. But it was hard. All night long Jacob prayed and wrestled with an angel of God. The angel touched Jacob's hip so he would limp. Then God blessed Jacob. When the sun came up, Jacob limped off to meet Esau.

As he came nearer to Esau, Jacob's heart pounded. His hands sweated. But he limped toward Esau and bowed low seven times. Then he looked at Esau. Esau came running toward him. Would Esau kill him?

Suddenly Jacob felt Esau's arms around him. They kissed. They hugged. They cried as tears raced down their faces. At long last they were brothers again. Jacob's sins were forgiven! Forgiven and gone forever!

Jacob was so happy to have his sins forgiven. That meant he could live with his brother in love again. And that's the way it is for us too. God doesn't want us to live far away from him. No! God loves us. He wants us to live with him in heaven some day. The next chapter tells us about God's great plan to save us.

3 The Good News

God's Perfect Son
(John 3:16, 17)

God loves us very much, even though He doesn't love our sins. He wanted to save us so we could live with him forever. The only way would be for someone to take our place; someone perfect, without sin; someone willing to take our punishment for us.

God has a Son. He loves this Son a lot. This Son never sinned, not even once!

God thought about our sins and His perfect Son. God decided on a plan to save us. He would send His Son, His only Son, to this world to take our place. That Son would have to live on earth, die, and suffer the pain of living apart from God.

Just think about this plan for a little while. Oh, how God loved His Son, but He loved us too. God loved us so much that He was willing to send His Son down to earth to give us clean hearts. What a wonderful God we have! The next stories will tell you how this exciting plan worked.

Earthly Parents for Jesus

(Luke 1:26–31)

God's Son would live in this world just as we do. He would need feet, hands, head, arms . . . a body like ours. And so God sent Him to this world as a baby. God was His Father. But a lady named Mary would be His mother. This baby would still be God like His Father. But He would be a regular person too, like His mother. He would be God and man together.

An angel came to Mary and said, "You are going to have a baby, and you will call him Jesus. I know you aren't married, but don't worry. God is the Father of this baby. Jesus is His Son." Then the angel left Mary alone to think.

Mary was excited. She was thrilled. She would be the mother of God's Son, baby Jesus! She was eager to tell her boyfriend, Joseph, the good news. They were planning to get married. Joseph would want to know.

When Joseph learned that Mary was going to have a baby he was a little worried. They weren't married yet. What would people say?

But God spoke to Joseph too. One night while he was sleeping and dreaming, one of God's angels came into his dreams. The angel said, "Joseph, don't be afraid. Mary is going to have God's Son, Jesus. He will save His people from their sins. Go ahead, you and Mary should get married."

Joseph felt much better about it now. God's son, Jesus, would have an earthly father to care for Him.

Joseph did what the angel said and took Mary as his wife.

After they were man and wife, Joseph and Mary were eager for this child to be born. Jesus, the Savior of men, would grow up in their home!

Born in a Manger
(Luke 2:1–7)

About six months later the governor sent out a law ordering everyone to go back to the city where they were born. He wanted to count the people so he knew how much tax money he should collect. This happened very close to the time Mary's baby was ready to be born. Traveling now would be hard.

But it was a command. Everyone had to go. So Joseph packed a few things and put Mary on a donkey. She couldn't walk far because the baby was so large. She rode the donkey while Joseph led the way.

They traveled for a long time, days and nights. It was about seventy-five miles. That's a very long ride, especially on a donkey. Ask your dad or mom how far that is. Wouldn't that be a long trip?

When Mary and Joseph arrived in Bethlehem they looked for a room to sleep in. But everyone they asked had no extra room. So many people were in town that every bed was filled!

Mary was tired. Joseph's feet burned from the long walk. They would have to stay somewhere. Finally one man said that they could sleep on the hay in his barn. Joseph and Mary were glad. At least they could sleep!

While they rested on the hay, they heard some cattle chewing their feed. Others were sleeping noisily. There were the sounds and smells of animals. It certainly wasn't fancy, but it was a place to rest.

That night, on the hay in the barn, God's Son was born. Baby Jesus, the Savior of all men, was born in a barn. God must have loved us a lot to send His only Son to be born in a barn. Instead of having doctors and nurses around Him, Baby Jesus was surrounded by cattle!

Mary wrapped some clothes around Him and laid Him in a box that held cattle feed. Imagine! Baby Jesus didn't even have a baby bed of His own. He was laid in a manger. And that's how Jesus came to this earth.

Frightened by an Angel

(Luke 2:8–14)

While Jesus was being born in the barn, the people in the houses nearby didn't even know it. But outside the city there was a lot of excitement.

There were shepherds caring for their sheep. The stars stood watch over the snoozing lambs. The shepherds lay on the hillside dozing. Every once in a while one would awaken to check that the flock was safe. Then he would doze off again. The country was quiet and restful.

Suddenly the shepherds jerked to attention. They were startled by a brilliant light. It was an angel . . . a real one! They covered their faces

quickly.
Their sleep-
ing eyes
weren't
ready for
light, espe-
cially not
such a
dazzling one.

For a
moment they
shook with fear.
They were just plain scared.
Should they run? Should they try to hide?

As they wondered what to do, the angel said, "Please don't be afraid. I've got good news for everyone! This very night Jesus, the Savior, has been born. You'll find Him lying in a manger."

Just as the angel stopped talking it seemed as if God pulled back the dark night curtain. For out of the heavens came a choir of angels. They were singing. They were happy. They sang loud praises to God! The hillsides buzzed with the glory and excitement. Christ, the Savior, was born!

Eager Visitors

(Luke 2:15–20)

When the angels had finished their singing they went back into heaven. The dark night sky covered the earth again. The shepherds were anxious. They couldn't hurry fast enough to see this baby. A couple of them might have stayed to care for the sheep. But surely most of them rushed off to the city. They were going to see the Savior.

As they came near the city, they started looking in barns. And sure enough, after peeking into different ones, they found Joseph, Mary, and Jesus. It was true!

It was all true! Here lay the baby Savior in a manger in front of their own eyes!

The shepherds talked excitedly. They told Joseph and Mary about what had happened on the hillside. Other people heard the chattering and came in to listen too. They talked about the angels, the singing, and what the angel messenger had said.

The good news of Jesus spread quickly. Many people came from around the city, hoping to see the Savior from sin. Such good news soon traveled throughout the whole town. Everybody heard about it.

People didn't have telephones and radios and televisions. But the news spread almost as fast. People couldn't wait to tell their neighbors and friends. This was good news!

A Perfect Child

(Luke 2:39–40)

Jesus' mother and father stayed in Bethlehem for a short time. Then they hurried off to Egypt to hide from King

Herod who was looking for this new baby King. After a few years they finally headed for Nazareth, their hometown.

Back in Nazareth Joseph got back to his work quickly. He was a carpenter. He probably had a lot of tables, chairs, and cabinets to make. He had been out of town for a long time. He must have been behind in his orders for furniture.

Mary was busy too. She had a little boy to take care of. And you know how much work little children can be. Don't you think that Joseph and Mary had fun seeing Jesus crawl around? Then He learned how to walk and talk. I'm sure they were very happy parents.

But there was one thing about Jesus

that was different from that of any other child. He never sinned. He was perfect, remember? He is the Son of God!

He didn't talk back to his parents. He always did what they asked Him to do. He didn't cry and pout if He didn't get His way. He shared His toys. Yes, He was a perfect child.

Lost and Found

(Luke 2:41–50)

The Bible doesn't tell us very much about Jesus when He was a little boy. The next time we read about Him He is twelve years old.

Joseph and Mary went to Jerusalem with many of their friends and their children. They went to celebrate a holiday. It was another long trip. Walking goes quite slowly, especially with little ones along.

When the feast and the celebration were over, the whole group started their journey home. The children were gathered. Everything was packed. The donkeys were lined up. Slowly the line started moving . . . back to Nazareth.

Joseph and Mary thought that Jesus was with the group of children. They didn't bother to check on Him. After all, He was twelve years old now. He could get along pretty well by Himself.

When the group stopped for the night, they looked for Jesus. They asked the other boys and girls. They asked their friends. But no one had seen Him. Jesus was missing!

Joseph and Mary left the others quickly. They went back to Jerusalem. It took a day to walk back. They asked in the city market and at the stores. They asked people standing in the streets. They asked children playing in the road. But for three days they heard nothing about Him. Joseph and Mary were frantic!

On the fourth day they went to the Temple. As they walked up the steps, they thought they heard a familiar voice. It sounded like their son. Could it be?

Was He still alive? They went into the back of the Temple. Sure enough! There sat Jesus talking with the ministers and teachers. They were talking about grown-up things. It was important talk. The men were amazed at this twelve-year-old child!

Mary hurried to Jesus and scolded Him, "So, why did you do this to us? We've been worried about you. We have been looking all over town."

Jesus answered His mother. But He answered her in a strange way. He said, "Why did you look for me? Don't you know that I am here to do my Father's work?"

His parents didn't really understand. Jesus did go back home with them. And He stayed with them for many years. But Jesus was trying to help them understand that He was really God's Son. His Heavenly Father would always come first. His Father had a plan for Him . . . a plan to save sinners.

A Loving Friend

(Luke 7:11–15; 9:12–17)

When Jesus was a grown man He started doing God's work full time. He left Joseph and Mary. He traveled from city to city. He told about God's love. He preached about sin. He told grown-ups and children to be sorry for sinning.

Jesus showed God's love by being kind. He did amazing things. We call them miracles. He raised a boy, a girl, and a man from the dead. Yes, He put life into their dead bodies.

He healed so many people! He fixed blind eyes to see. He straightened weak and wobbly legs. People with rotting skin were healed.

He made tangy red wine out of regular water. That was the first miracle that

The Good News

He did. He also fed five thousand people from just five biscuits and two fish. Wonderful, isn't it?

Jesus was a storyteller . . . the best! So many people and children loved to hear Him. They would sit on the side of the hills while He told God's stories. He talked to people about doing wrong things. He asked them to love God. Jesus came to this earth to take away the sins of everyone who would believe. This was all part of God's plan to have us live with him forever, remember?

The Friendly Enemy

(Matthew 26:20–25)

Not everyone Jesus met loved Him. There were some who hated Him. They didn't like to hear about their sins. They thought they were perfect. They were enemies of Jesus. They wouldn't listen to Him. They wouldn't obey Him and they wouldn't love Him. They didn't want other people to love Jesus, either.

Everywhere Jesus went He met some who believed and some who didn't. He told them that He was the King. He was the Savior from sin.

Some people thought He would be a king on earth. They thought He would have a palace and a throne. They just didn't understand that He was a heavenly king.

One of Jesus' enemies was a close friend. In fact, he was one of the twelve men that Jesus loved most. They were called the twelve disciples.

Just before the time when Jesus would die for our sins, He had His friends together for supper. While they were eating Jesus surprised them. He said, "Someone is going to take me to be killed. It is one of you, my friends."

They were almost too shocked to answer. They all thought, "Kill you, Jesus? We love you too much."

Finally when they could speak they called out, "Who is it, Lord? Is it I? Will I be the one to do such a terrible thing?"

Even the very man who was going to do it said, "Jesus, am I the one?" His name was Judas.

Jesus looked right at him and answered, "Judas, you have said it. You are the one."

When Jesus said that, Judas grabbed his things. He ran out quickly. He thought, "How does Jesus know? How can He tell my sinful heart? How, how, could He tell?"

And Jesus was right. He knew exactly what had happened. Judas had taken thirty pieces of silver. That would be about twenty dollars today. That was his pay. He was going to sell Jesus to be killed.

Sold by a Kiss

(Matthew 26:36–50)

After Judas left the supper table, Jesus and his friends went out to the garden. Jesus wanted to be alone with His friends and His Father. He knew that during this night He would be taken. Judas and the enemies would soon arrive.

Jesus asked His disciples to stay and pray. He wanted to talk to God about their plan to save men. But while Jesus prayed, His friends slept. Three times Jesus had to wake them up.

Suddenly they heard the clatter of swords. A small army of men was coming. Judas was with them. He was ready to do his trick. He was ready to kiss Jesus. That way the soldiers would know which man to grab.

Judas came to Jesus and said, "Master!" Then he quickly kissed Jesus on the cheek. He had earned his money. He did his job. He sold Jesus for a kiss!

The soldiers had their man. They were enemies of Jesus. At last they captured Him. Now they hoped to kill Him.

While Jesus was taken away, where do you think His friends were? They were scared. They saw soldiers and swords. Off they ran! They left Jesus with the enemy.

In the Courtroom

(Matthew 27:19–26)

Jesus had to have a trial. His enemies couldn't just kill Him. So they took Him to court. They said things about Him that

weren't true. They were hoping to make Jesus seem like a very bad man.

Jesus listened to their angry words. He was very quiet. He was sad because people didn't understand

that He came to earth because He loves us.

Next Jesus was taken to Pilate, the governor. Pilate asked Jesus questions. He listened carefully to what Jesus said. He didn't think that Jesus should die.

But the crowd wanted Him to die. They kept calling, "Kill Him! Kill Him!"

The people were so angry. They screamed. They hollered. They shouted. They were crazy with hate for Jesus. Finally Pilate said, "I can't find anything wrong with this man. But I will give you a choice. We will let one man go free. Let Jesus free or let Barabbas free."

Barabbas was a robber and a killer. Pilate was sure that the people wouldn't want this bad man running free. But the people cried and screamed even louder, "Give us Barabbas!"

Pilate washed his hands. He didn't think Jesus was evil. But the people were filled with anger. So Jesus would be killed.

Making Fun of Jesus

(Matthew 27:27–32)

Pilate gave Jesus to the soldiers. They took off most of His clothes. They beat Jesus. Then they put a purple coat on Him. Someone made a crown out of thorny twigs. They put that on His head. It hurt. But Jesus was quiet. He didn't say a word. Jesus took all of this for us ... for your sins and mine. He loves us!

Then they gave Jesus a stick to hold. They were pretending He was a king. They laughed and giggled. Some even bowed down in front of Him. They called, "Hail, King of the Jews!"

92   **The Good News**

Others spit in His face. One man took the stick and poked at His head. Oh, what fun they had. How mean they were. God's perfect Son, Jesus, took it all. He said nothing while they beat Him.

Perfect Jesus didn't deserve this.

You did.

I did.

But Jesus took it for us.

Then they put His own clothes back on Him. They led Him away to be killed. Jesus was made to carry the cross on which He would die. The cross was very heavy, and it was a long way to the hill where robbers and bad men were nailed to crosses so they would die. Jesus became so weak that He couldn't carry His cross anymore.

Just then a big, strong man named Simon happened to come along. The soldiers forced him to carry Jesus' cross.

The Darkest Day

(Matthew 27:33–38)

When they came to a hill called Calvary, Simon laid the cross down. Jesus was laid on it. Then the soldiers pounded nails into his hands and feet. The men dug the round, deep hole. Then that big cross with Jesus on it was put into the hole. The cross was pushed high in the air.

There hung Jesus. He was nailed to a cross of wood. The soldiers put a sign over His head. It said:

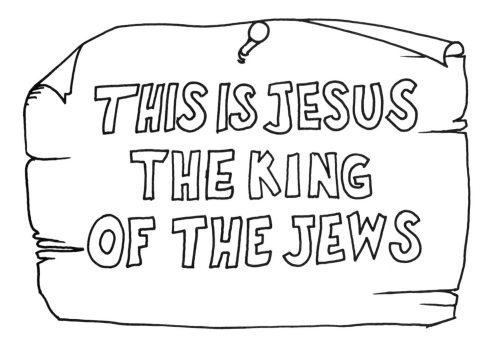

THIS IS JESUS THE KING OF THE JEWS

Two other men were killed that day. They were robbers. They deserved to be punished. But Jesus, the perfect Son of God, didn't. No, He was there because of our sins.

The worst part came next. God left His only Son alone. To have His heavenly Father forsake Him was a terrible, terrible punishment. And Jesus took all this punishment for us! He died for us because He loved us so much.

The Brightest Day

(Matthew 27:57–66; 28:1–8)

When Jesus died the sky became coal black. The ground shook. The curtain in the Temple ripped from the top to the bottom. Graves were opened. Many people that were watching were afraid. Now they knew Jesus really was the Son of God.

Later that day one of Jesus' friends came to get the body. He wrapped it in white cloths. He buried Jesus in his own grave. It was in the side of a rocky hill. Then he rolled a big stone in front of it and left.

But Pilate was afraid. He had let God's Son be killed. He thought Jesus might escape. Or some of His friends might steal the body. So he ordered guards to watch the grave.

Early Sunday morning two women came to visit the grave. But just as they got there the ground shook very hard.

Houses rattled. The rocks jiggled. And an angel pushed the stone away from the grave.

Jesus' body was gone! The grave was just plain empty! No body! No Jesus! He had risen from the grave just as God had planned.

Heaven and Home

(Luke 24:50–52; Revelation 3:20)

Jesus met many of His friends and disciples. How happy they were to see Him. Their Jesus was alive again. They talked excitedly. They thought He would stay on earth and live with them.

But Jesus was going to go back to live with His Father. He had been on earth for thirty-three years. He wanted to return to heaven.

One day as He was walking with them He gave them a blessing. As he finished blessing them His body began to float up from the ground. Higher and higher He went. Slowly He rose until His head went into the clouds. Then His feet disappeared. Finally Jesus had disappeared completely! Jesus was living in heaven again.

This part of God's plan was over. His Son Jesus did everything that needed to be done on this earth. That's why you and I can go to heaven one day if we believe God and love Him.

Jesus now lives in heaven, but He can also live in you. You only have to close your eyes and pray. Ask Jesus to come into your heart and live in you. If you pray this prayer, God will come in because He promised it. He said, "And it shall come to pass, that whosoever shall call on the name of the Lord, shall be saved" (Acts 2:21).

4 Acts of Hate

The First Murder

(Genesis 4:1–12)

The Bible, God's Book, tells us about some people who listened to Satan. Others listened to God and obeyed Him. This chapter tells us about people who hated.

Adam and Eve had two sons named Cain and Abel. Cain was the older boy who grew up to be a farmer. How long he worked planting tiny seeds! When they were dry he had to carry water from the streams to the thirsty young plants. He spent many hours on his knees pulling out the tough weeds that tried to strangle the tender new shoots.

Abel chose to care for sheep. Every day he carefully led his flock to green, moist grass. As they nudged and nibbled their supper, Abel sang to them. But his eyes and ears were looking and listening for a hungry animal which might harm one of his little ones. They were very precious to him.

Satan worked very hard on these two young men. How often he came to them and urged them not to praise God. Sometimes he laughed at them. He stayed very close to them, hoping to keep God out of their hearts.

One day the two brothers brought offerings to God. Cain brought some of the fruit of his garden. Abel brought a young lamb, one of his fattest and

best. Both of them put their offerings on the altar.

God looked down upon these offerings. But He also looked at the hearts of the young men who gave them. Abel's heart was thankful. He loved God. He had not listened to Satan. But Cain's heart did not love God. He had listened to Satan. When he brought his offering he wasn't even thinking of God and His goodness.

God said that He was very happy with Abel's offering because Abel's heart was loving. But God was angry with Cain for giving an offering when his heart wasn't even given with it. So God told Cain that He was very unhappy with him. He saw that Satan had entered his heart.

Cain was furious because his offering was not accepted. As he thought about it, he became jealous of his brother. Finally Cain began to hate Abel. Then Cain planned to do something very, very wrong. He waited for Abel in the field. And when he thought no one was looking, he killed his own brother, Abel. Then Cain hurried away, hoping no one saw him do it.

But God saw what Cain had done. He called to Cain asking, "Where is Abel, your brother?"

"I don't know," Cain called back. "Am I supposed to take care of him?"

God answered, "I saw what you did. Now I am going to punish you. You will have to spend the rest of your life running from place to place. But I will still care for you, Cain. I won't let anyone kill you as you have killed your brother." And on that day, Cain began his journey to a faraway country.

A Brother for Sale!
(Genesis 37:12–36)

A man named Jacob had many children. One of his children whom he liked very much was Joseph. He liked Joseph so much that he gave him a beautiful coat that was striped with many different colors.

Joseph's brothers began to hate him. They did this for two reasons. One was the lovely coat. It was more fancy than the coats Jacob had given them. And they became jealous because Joseph had many special dreams which meant that someday he would rule over all the brothers. Whenever Joseph told them about his dreams the brothers laughed and called him "The Dreamer." They hated him so much that they couldn't even talk nicely to him.

Father Jacob owned flocks of sheep. The older boys had to take these sheep far away where they could find tender grass. Sometimes the boys had to stay overnight because it was too far to come home. Whenever this happened Jacob worried about them.

One day when the brothers had been away for a little while, Jacob asked

Joseph, "Will you go and find your brothers for me? See how they are. Ask about the sheep. Then hurry home. I'm so anxious to hear about them." Joseph was happy to do these errands for his father. Before he left he put on his coat, the coat of many colors. Then he started out to find his brothers.

As Joseph came near the place where the brothers were, they noticed him coming. One laughingly said, "Hey, fellows! Here comes Dreamer Boy. I've got an idea. Let's kill him. All right?"

But the oldest brother said, "I don't think we should kill him. If you want to get rid of him, just throw him into that deep hole over there." All the brothers quickly agreed. And when Joseph got close to them, they ripped off his coat and put him in the pit before he could even ask them how they were.

Then the brothers sat down to eat. As they ate they talked about Joseph and what they should do with him. If they left him in the hole, he would surely starve to death.

Just as they were talking about this, they saw a group of men coming. They were rich men who bought and sold things. This would solve their problems. They would sell Joseph!

And they did exactly that. They sold him to be a servant boy. Soon Joseph was on his way to a strange, new country where he knew no one.

The brothers didn't dare to tell Father Jacob about their hating and selling Joseph. So they killed a lamb from their flock and put Joseph's beautiful coat in the blood. When they gave the bloody coat to Jacob they said, "See what we found? It was in the road. A wild animal must have killed Joseph." Not only did they hate, they also had lied to cover up their wicked deed.

A Jealous King

(1 Samuel 19:8–10)

King Saul was a jealous king. He was jealous of a young man in his kingdom. He disliked the lad because he could do so many things better than the King himself. He was an army officer who won many battles. He was a very good musician. And so many people in the kingdom learned to love him. Even King Saul's own children and servants loved this young man whose name was David.

When the King knew that the people in his kingdom loved David more than him, he became angry, so angry in fact, that he planned to kill David. How carefully he planned this! He invited David to the palace and asked him to play a song for him on the harp. While David's fingers were running over the musical strings, King Saul pulled out his long hunting spear. He aimed carefully and quickly. Then in a moment he flung it straight toward David. King Saul was hoping to get rid of this young man forever.

But David was very alert. Out of the corner of his eye he had seen what the King was doing. He jumped off his stool just in time to save his life. Quickly David left the palace.

For many years David had to run from Saul because Saul's heart was so full of evil hatred for him. After Saul was an older man he asked David to forgive him for this sin. At last David no longer had to run from the hating heart of King Saul.

Tricked into a Lions' Den
(Daniel 6:1–24)

Daniel was a man whose heart was filled with love for God. He lived a good life and did his work very carefully. He was kind and loving toward those who worked for him. That is why most people liked him. King Darius liked him so very much that he decided to name Daniel as the most important man under himself. He called Daniel the First President.

Can you imagine what an important position this was? There were other men in the kingdom who wanted this job. When they heard that Daniel got the job instead of one of them, they became jealous. By now you know that when people get jealous they often do sinful things. And that is just what happened to these men.

One day they got together to make a plan against Daniel. He was such a godly man they knew it would be almost impossible to catch him doing something wrong. They also knew that Daniel prayed to God every day.

When their plan was carefully worked out they went to the King and said, "King Darius, live forever! You are such a good king that we have decided to make a law saying that everyone must worship you and only you for the next thirty days. And if anyone should be caught praying to another god, we will throw him immediately into the lions' den."

King Darius thought for a moment about this law. He could find nothing wrong with it, so he signed the paper and their wicked plan became a law. The men were thrilled! Have you figured out how their plan will work? Do they really like the King so much? Or are they trying to get rid of Daniel?

Even though Daniel heard about this law, he knew he could not pray to King Darius. Though Darius was a nice man and Daniel liked the King, he was not God. So Daniel opened his windows and

Acts of Hate

prayed to the Lord God just as he always did, three times each day.

The plan had worked. Daniel's enemies saw him praying to God, and they hurried to the King. When the King heard what Daniel had done, he realized he had been tricked. He loved Daniel so. But the law could not be changed.

The guards were called to bring Daniel, and he was put into a den full of hungry, angry lions. A big stone was rolled in front of the den and the hole was sealed shut.

That night the King was so unhappy. One of his best men, his friend, was surely dead by now. All night long the King worried about Daniel. That's right. King Darius didn't sleep a wink!

That same night the men who had planned this trick were overjoyed. They were rid of Daniel at last! Now one of them could be made First President of the kingdom. They laughed to think of how easily their plan had worked.

When the King got up in the morning he hurried to the lions' den. He listened. He couldn't hear Daniel. Everything was deathly still. The King's heart saddened. But, just to be sure, he shouted, "Daniel, Oh, Daniel. Did your God save you?" King Darius really didn't expect an answer. He was sure that Daniel was dead.

But Daniel called out, "Oh, King Darius. My God sent an angel to close the mouth of every lion here. Not one of them has bitten me. I'm not even scratched!"

The King's mouth dropped open. He couldn't believe his own ears. Daniel, alive? He was so thrilled that he lost no time in calling men to pry the stone from the door of the den. And when the King looked in he saw Daniel sitting right in the middle of all the lions. They were lying around him like gentle, purring kittens. What a powerful God! Daniel was saved!

The men who hated Daniel and thought of this wicked plan were punished. King Darius threw them into the lions' den.

Stones for Love

(Acts 7:54–60)

The Bible tells about a missionary whose name was Stephen. He was a very busy man who loved God and worked hard for Him. Stephen preached to many people. He healed their sicknesses. He told them about Jesus so their hearts could become clean. Whenever he talked to people, some wanted a new heart and a new life.

But there were some men in the city where Stephen was preaching who did not love God. They didn't want others to love God either. Their hearts were given to Satan. So they waited for a chance to get Stephen into trouble.

They listened to him preach. They watched him. How eagerly they hoped to find something wrong. But they could find nothing. They would have to lie about things Stephen did. They sent men to tell the rulers that Stephen was making fun of God Himself! Now isn't that a strange lie to tell? Stephen loved the Lord. Would he laugh at the God he loved? Of course not! He would only speak the truth.

Because of this lie Stephen was

brought to the courtroom. The men repeated their lie and then Stephen was given a chance to answer them. But Stephen didn't even try because the lie seemed so foolish.

Instead Stephen began to preach to the rulers, the men who had lied, and to all others in the courtroom. Everyone listened closely. Stephen talked about God. He told the truth. The men who thought of the lies and the men who had told them became uncomfortable. The longer they listened the more angry they became. When they could stand it no longer they grabbed Stephen, even while he was standing and preaching. They dragged him out of the courtroom and down the streets of the city.

When they arrived outside the city they took off their coats. They wanted nothing to stop them or get in their way. They were determined to kill this man!

They looked for rocks, not little stones.

As quickly as they found them they threw them at Stephen. And while they threw stones at him, Stephen prayed: "Lord Jesus, receive my spirit." And then Stephen died. He was killed by people with hate in their hearts.

5 Deeds of Love

A Traveling Friend

(Luke 10:30–37)

Hearts can hate, but hearts can also love. Some stories from the Bible tell about hearts that love God and men.

This story is one that Jesus told. It is about a man who was taking a trip. He was walking along the road on his way to Jericho. Just as he turned a corner, robbers jumped out from behind and pounced

on him. They grabbed his wallet, ripped his clothes, and left him in the road alone. He was bleeding badly and needed care quickly.

Soon a priest came down the same road. A priest is the head of a church, a minister. When he saw the wounded man he quickly crossed the street so he wouldn't have to look at his beaten body. Surely the heart of this priest did not love.

Then a Levite came. He noticed something lying in the road. Why, it looked like a man's body! When he realized that it was a person, he quickly crossed the street, just as the priest had done. Can

you imagine that? A priest, the head of the church, didn't help and a Levite, the priest's helper, didn't help either. They talked about love in their churches but their hearts did not love.

Then a man from Samaria came by on his donkey. He is called the Samaritan. He glanced ahead. "A man lying in the middle of the road?" he

Deeds of Love

asked himself. When he reached the man he saw how badly he was wounded. Quickly and tenderly he poured wine and soothing oils on his bleeding sores, wrapped the cuts and bruises. Carefully he lifted the man onto his donkey and walked into the next city.

When they arrived the Samaritan looked for an inn. He left the donkey at the animals' stall and carefully carried the wounded man to a room. This man needed so much rest and care. Again he checked all the sores to be doubly sure he would be all right for the night. Soon both men were fast asleep.

In the morning the Samaritan paid for the rooms. To the inn manager he said, "Please take very good care of this man. I know it'll cost a lot of money. But I will surely pay you the next time I come to your city."

How can you tell which man in this story had a heart full of love? He even loved a stranger. That is why this man is called the "Good Samaritan."

Ninety-Nine Plus One

(Luke 15:1–7)

Jesus tells us many stories in the Bible. Another one about love is called "The Good Shepherd." This shepherd had exactly one hundred sheep. He knew them just as well as mothers know their children. By looking at the way they held their ears and tails, the spots on their bodies, their eyes, or the way they walked, he knew just which one was which. The sheep, too, could tell the shepherd's voice from others.

You know how mothers tuck their little ones in at night. This shepherd did the same with his sheep. As he let them under the gate and into the fold, he counted each one to be certain all came back with him at night.

And every night when the last sheep was in, he had reached one hundred. Then the shepherd himself could lie down and sleep peacefully because all of his flock were safely home.

But one evening he had reached only ninety-nine when the last sheep was counted. His heart pounded and he got a lump in his throat. "Oh, no! One of my sheep is missing!" his heart cried. And he counted them again, so carefully. But again he counted only ninety-nine.

It took only a moment for him to decide that he must look for the little lamb. He knew exactly which one was the missing sheep. Quickly he left the fold.

He climbed the rolling hills and walked through scratching briar patches. He slipped on rocks that led down to deep ditches. As he walked he called to his lost sheep. Then he stopped so he could listen

in complete silence. But no answer came. Then he would walk a little farther and call again, hoping for an answer.

The shepherd in this story is called the "Good Shepherd." He was good because he didn't stop looking  even though he knew that he still had ninety-nine back in the fold. The hills were rocky and dangerous but he kept wandering, searching, and calling. Finally he heard a faint, Baa-a-a. He stopped and listened for the direction of that tired sheep cry. Quickly he started toward the sound.

When he found his little sheep he carefully put the frightened lamb in his arms and started for the fold. At last the lost was found! The shepherd was weak and his bones ached from climbing and walking in the darkness of the night. But his flock would be together again—all one hundred of them.

Sometimes Jesus is called the Good Shepherd too. He loves every girl and boy so much that he is willing to look for them and give them clean, loving hearts.

Perfume for Jesus
(John 12:1–8)

Mary loved Jesus so much. She became so excited whenever He was coming to visit and stay for supper. For this evening she had gotten something very special because she wanted to show Jesus that she really loved Him. It was very expensive perfume. It cost so much that Mary must have saved a long time for it.

While all the guests were at the supper table, Mary got the costly perfume and poured it, all of it, over Jesus' feet. Then she wiped His feet with her hair. Just think, Mary was willing to spend that

much money just to wipe the feet of her friend, Jesus.

No sooner had she done this then Judas, one of the guests who loved money, jumped to his feet and shouted, "Mary, how stupid of you! That perfume could have been sold for $48. At least you could have given the money to the poor!"

But Jesus said, "Quiet, Judas. Leave Mary alone. She has done this because she loves me."

6 Acts of Unbelief

A Special Promise

(Genesis 18:1–15)

Abraham and Sarah leaned back in their outdoor chairs. They were getting old and they often sat outside in front of their tent house and watched the children who tussled and tumbled around their yard. Maybe the reason they liked to see little ones so much was because they had no children of their own.

Hundreds of cattle and sheep grazed and wandered on the many acres of land Abraham owned. He and Sarah were very rich and could buy most anything they wanted. But they couldn't buy a child. Besides, they were old and gray now. They knew that God doesn't usually give tiny babies to older people. So they tried to forget how much they wanted a baby of their very own.

Late in the afternoon of a scorching day Abraham saw some men coming to his tent. They looked like visitors so he ran out to say hello. He gave them water to wash their dusty, tired feet and invited them to sit in the shade of a large, leafy tree.

Perhaps you serve a cold drink or tea or coffee to guests that stop in for a chat. But Abraham told Sarah to prepare a feast... fresh cakes, tender young beef, creamy butter, and cool milk.

Abraham knew that these were special men. They were messengers of God!

While the guests and Abraham ate this tasty food, the messengers told him something quite surprising. They said, "Abraham, your wife is going to have a baby boy."

Sarah stood just inside the tent. She happened to hear what the men had said. Before she could think, she laughed and thought, "Me? Have a baby? Can't be! I'm too old!"

You may be surprised to learn that Sarah loved God. But Satan kept working in her heart. He tried to get Sarah to think that God couldn't do hard jobs like giving a baby to an older lady. Satan's plan worked. Sarah laughed. She thought that God surely couldn't do this!

But God showed Sarah that He meant

just what He had said. When it was exactly time, Sarah had a baby ... and it was a boy! Abraham and Sarah named him Isaac. They were so very happy to have a son. How sorry Sarah must have been that she had laughed about God's promise.

Complaining People
(Numbers 20:1–11)

The Israelites were God's special people. He chose them to be His own and He cared for them. One time God led them into the desert to live. While they were living there, they lived in tents.

Tent living in the desert can be quite uncomfortable, you know. They had to eat whatever food they could find, perhaps only wild berries. They cooked in large pots over an open fire. If it rained the ground was muddy and slippery. If they had no rain for many days it became very hot and stuffy. Drinking water was hard to find.

You may wonder why God would take His chosen people to such a place. He did it because He was leading His people to a new and beautiful place to live. They had to travel by foot to get there. There were no airplanes or trains in those days.

And so they traveled step by step by step. Once they couldn't find water where they stopped to camp. Another time they could find no food, no wild berries, absolutely nothing! The people went to their leader and nagged and cried, "Why, O why, did God ever bring us to this place?" You see, they weren't trusting God. They thought that God wouldn't take care of them.

Maybe you're thinking that you would complain too. "After all," you say, "if I was hungry, thirsty, dusty, and my feet were sore from walking, I think I'd complain a little too."

Just in case you're thinking that, think about how the Israelites lived before God led them away.

It was in a land where they were made slaves. It was a hot country where people made buildings from mud bricks. The Israelites had to make these bricks, one by one. If they didn't work fast enough, the Egyptians beat them to make them hustle a bit faster. When they did work just as fast as they possibly could, the work masters expected them to make even more bricks the next time. Sometimes they worked and sweated under the broiling sun until they fainted! But the king of the land didn't feel sorry for them. They had to keep making bricks.

Yet there had been something even worse than being treated so badly by their masters. That was the time the king of the land sent his messengers to every Israelite house to check for baby boys. The king was very cruel and didn't want any Israelite baby boys to live. It broke the fathers' and mothers' hearts to watch the messengers take away their precious baby boys.

Now do you understand why the Israelites had no reason to complain? God had taken them out of that land of miserable slavery. Living in the desert surely wasn't the most pleasant place, but think how much better it was than being beaten and killed!

The Israelites had no reason to believe that God wouldn't care for them, did they? When there was no water, God opened a rock and out bubbled fresh, clean water. When they were hungry God sent bread from heaven. God did take care of His people.

A Man Who Couldn't Talk

(Luke 1:11–22, 57–64)

Have you ever met anyone who couldn't talk? Someone besides a little baby? That is exactly the problem that

Zacharias, a priest in the Temple, had. Oh, yes, he could twist his tongue. His jaw moved easily when he ate. And even his lips moved. But whenever he wanted to speak, not a sound would come . . . not even a squeak or a whisper!

Zacharias wasn't born with this problem. He was an old man and he had had this only a short time. He couldn't speak because God had punished him.

Zacharias and his wife, Elizabeth, were old and had no children—just like Abraham and Sarah. An angel of God came before him and said, "Your wife is going to have a little boy. And when he is born, you shall name him John. He will grow up to love God and will help do the Lord's work."

Zacharias was shocked at what he heard. He looked at the angel and questioned, "How can I be sure that this will really happen? You know that Elizabeth and I are very old."

God was disappointed in this man. He didn't believe God just as Sarah had not. So God punished him by not allowing him to speak until after the baby was born. Wherever Zacharias went he carried writing materials with

him. If someone asked him a question, he wrote the answer. What a bother that must have been! Can you imagine writing down every single word that you say in a whole day? at the table? at school? a ball game? What a chore!

When Elizabeth's baby was born, Zacharias couldn't speak right away. He still carried his materials with him. It was when the baby was eight days old that God gave his voice back to him.

Zacharias and Elizabeth took the baby to the Temple to promise his life to God. The relatives and friends were there with them. When it was time to name the baby, everyone said that his name should be Zacharias, like his father.

But Elizabeth immediately said, "No, we are going to name him John."

"John?" everyone asked, quite surprised. "Nobody in your whole family is named John." They looked at Zacharias as if to say, "Do you want him to be named John?"

Zacharias quickly wrote, "His name will be John."

The very second he wrote this God gave him back his voice. Zacharias told all the people how good God was for giving them this little boy even when they were very old.

7 Deeds of Faith

An Unusual Baby Basket

(Exodus 2:1–10)

"A baby boy," the family whispered. They looked at each other in quick, nervous glances. Each one was thinking, "Where can we hide him? How can we keep him from crying? Hurry, or the king's messengers will hear!"

"That's strange," you say. "Why hide the baby? Is there something wrong with it? When a baby is born in our family we can't wait to tell our friends and relatives. Why are these people so worried? Why don't they want the king's messengers to hear the baby crying?"

This little baby boy was Moses. He was born to an Israelite family who loved and trusted God. But the king of their land was wicked. He made a law that all Israelite boy babies must be thrown into the river. Naturally they didn't want to drown their baby. So they hid him.

Hiding a baby isn't easy, especially when it cries so long and loud. You know how noisy little babies can be. That's why the family kept all their windows and doors closed. They hurried to rock or feed him whenever he cried. And it worked . . . at least for three months.

Now the baby was so big that they couldn't hide him any longer. Mother had to think of another way. She prayed and asked God to help her find a way to keep her little baby boy alive. She trusted God and God gave her an idea.

She walked by the river for a special reason. She was looking for the long reeds that grow there. She picked enough, then hurried home where she weaved a little basket. She covered it with mud and with tar so it wouldn't leak. It was very important that this little basket didn't leak, because she was going to float her baby in the river. When the basket was ready she tenderly put the baby in it.

Sneaking the basket to the river was a difficult job. Each member of the family walked back and forth to the river making sure there were no guards near. When the path seemed safe, Mother quickly carried her precious baby to the river and put him in the weeds that grew near the edge. The younger sister, Miriam, stayed nearby. She pretended to be playing, but all the while she kept her eye on the little basket in which her little brother was lying.

Later that day the king's daughter came to the river for her daily bath. She waded into the water, enjoying its coolness. She noticed the unusual little basket and sent one of her maidens to get it. Curiously she looked in to find the Israelite baby boy. As soon as she saw him, she loved him.

Miriam, who was really watching that little basket every second, ran to the

water's edge and called to the princess, "Would you like me to find a lady to take care of your little boy?" The princess called back, "I certainly would! Will you find someone for me?"

Miriam hardly waited for her to answer. She jumped over the weeds and ran straight to her mother. When she got home she was so out of breath she could hardly tell the good news.

When Miriam's mother heard what had happened, she thanked God for helping her. Now she would be able to take care of her own baby boy, even though he now belonged to the princess. She could let him play outside, tumble, scream, and somersault. The guards wouldn't dare harm the son of the princess!

Five Stones and a Giant

(1 Samuel 17:4–11, 38–51)

The Israelites were in the middle of a battle. And they were worried. Their enemy had an excellent soldier. He was a giant whose name was Goliath. Every morning and evening he came to the edge of the battle line and shouted, "What's the matter? Are you guys afraid of me? Send someone over to fight me. If he can kill me, we'll be your slaves. But if I kill him, you'll be our slaves."

Whenever Goliath roared like this the Israelites worried all the more. Those men who went to see Goliath turned around and ran. He was huge! He stood about nine and one-half feet tall. Who, just who, could they find who would dare to fight this monstrous man?

While they were discussing this problem, a little brother of several of the soldiers came with food from their father. This young boy was David. He listened to their worried voices. He had also heard the giant's teasing.

He boldly said, "I'm not afraid of that giant. I am on God's side. He'll take care of me and help me. I'll get out my slingshot and look for just the right stones." Off he ran, looking.

The soldiers worried about David. He was so young and so small. They didn't trust God to take care of little David. But David was so determined, they let him go to meet Goliath.

As David walked toward the giant everyone on both sides held their breath. There was a deathly silence ... until the giant laughed out loud. He teased and hollered, "What do you think I am? A dog? All you have is a little stick to fight with." Goliath's angry words echoed across the valley.

But David's knees didn't even shake. He shouted right back. "Maybe you do have a hunting spear and a lot of other weapons, but I've got God with me and God will help me kill you." While David talked he kept walking toward the giant. He was not afraid.

When the moment was right, David took out his slingshot, put a stone in it,

and whirled it around. In an instant a smooth little stone went whirring through the air. It hit Goliath right in the head and he fell crashing and clanging to the ground. Goliath was dead. David put his trust in God and God helped him.

Three in a Fire

(Daniel 3)

The musical instruments sounded. The music could be heard for miles. People rushed out of their homes and fell on their knees to worship the king's image. It was massive! The golden idol stood about ninety-five feet  high and was nine feet wide. Can you imagine how big that is?

The king had ordered everyone who could hear the music to fall on their knees and worship this idol. Anyone who refused would be thrown into a furnace of fire. The king had sent the message to everyone. And almost everyone obeyed.

One day messengers of the king arrived to report, "Oh, king! There are three men who will not worship your new image. They just refuse to do it!"

The king flew into a rage and demanded, "Bring those men to me immediately."

In a short time the messengers returned with the three men: Shadrach, Meshach, and Abednego. They were brought before the king, who shouted, "Is it true that you do not worship my golden image?" As he spoke his face grew purple-red with anger.

"It's true, O king," the three men answered. "Our God lives in heaven. We

trust Him to save us from the furnace of fire. And He can save us from you. We cannot worship your golden image. We will worship only the true God."

The king was furious! How would anyone dare to disobey him? He would punish them. And he would do it quickly. The king decided to show the people that no one could disobey him! The king shrieked, "Heat the furnace hotter and throw these men in!"

Shadrach, Meshach, and Abednego

were tied tightly and thrown into the middle of the furnace.

The men who had thrown them in were trapped by the heat and the flames. They fainted and fell to the ground. In a minute they were dead.

And Shadrach, Meshach, and Abednego? How were they? They could hardly be seen through the thick and wiggling smoke. But the king came to look. He strained his eyes in disbelief. What? Four men? Frantically he called to the guards. "Didn't we throw three men into the fire? Weren't they bound with ropes? I see four men ... and they're walking around! One man looks almost ... almost like the Son of God! Guards! Guards! Hurry! Look! Do you see what I see?"

The king and his men rushed near the fire. The king called, "Shadrach, Meshach, Abednego! Come out of the fire!"

The three men walked out of the fire and toward the king. Their hair wasn't touched! Their clothes weren't black and ragged. And even more amazing, they didn't even smell like smoke!

When the king saw them, he turned toward the aston- ished people and spoke, "The God of Shadrach, Meshach, and Abednego is a powerful God. He sent His angel to

care for these men. Never, no never, say a word against their God. For no other God can do such miracles!"

Just a Touch

(Mark 5:25–34)

She listened hopefully to her friend who told her about a man named Jesus. He had been healing so many people, some who couldn't walk, some who were blind, and He had even brought a dead man back to life. "Can it be true?" she excitedly asked her friend. "These are miracles indeed. When will He come to our town? If I only could see Him, I know He would make me well!"

For twelve years this woman had had a bleeding disease. She had traveled many miles and seen many doctors. But none could heal her. All her money was gone and now she was even feeling worse. She had to see Jesus! She believed that He could help her.

When she heard that Jesus was visiting the city, she got up very early in the morning to be certain not to miss Him. "This could be the most important day of my life," she thought to herself. Though she was weak from bleeding, she left her home and hurried toward town.

As she entered the streets of the city she saw crowds of people pushing and shoving. Jesus just had  to be somewhere in the middle of all those people. She walked to the edge of the crowd and began slowly pushing her way toward Jesus.

The closer she came to Him, the harder it was to move. People were pushed so tightly together. It was impossible to budge them. Each one seemed like a solid, immovable pole. She dropped to her knees hoping that she could touch His clothes. Even that would help her to be healed of her bleeding.

Stretching her arm just as far as she could, she touched the very bottom of His coat. At the same moment she felt the blood stop flowing. But before she could even get up she heard Jesus ask, "Who touched me?"

Jesus' friends answered with disgust, "How can you tell who touched you? There are so many people pushing against you that it would be impossible to say."

"Oh, no" Jesus said, looking around. "Someone touched my clothes. I could feel healing power go out of my body."

Frightened, the woman confessed, "Lord, I touched you. I wanted to be rid

of this bleeding. I just knew you could heal me." Smiling down at her, Jesus said, "Go home and be happy. Because you trusted me I've healed your body. And I've given you a clean heart."

A Big Surprise for a Little Man

(Luke 19:1–10)

Zacchaeus sat with his head in his hands. He was thinking about a problem he had. Today was the day that Jesus was coming to town. Wherever Jesus went there were such large crowds that it was very hard to push through to see Him. And, to make things even worse, Zacchaeus was a very little man. He was almost like some of the little people you may have seen.

As he sat there thinking, he got a brainstorm. "That's it," he shouted as he jumped up. "That's exactly what I'll do! I'll climb a tree."

He began looking for the perfect one. Not just any tree would do. At last he found a sycamore tree that seemed just right. It was next to the road that Jesus would use. He scrambled up to the biggest branch that leaned over the road. He wiggled around until he felt comfortable. Then he waited.

In a short time he heard voices from a

distance. He peeked through the leaves and looked. Sure enough! He could see the huge crowd. They were coming straight down the road, right toward him. Zacchaeus was so excited. He watched them come closer and closer. Soon he could see Jesus Himself.

Just as Jesus came to the tree, He looked right at Zacchaeus and said, "Zacchaeus, hurry, come down from that tree. I'm coming to your house for supper."

Zacchaeus couldn't believe what he heard. He was so surprised that he almost lost his balance. As fast as he could, he tumbled down and took Jesus to his home.

As they ate supper Jesus told Zacchaeus that if he believed that Jesus would clean his heart from sin he would go to heaven someday. Zacchaeus answered, "I do believe. I do. I do."

Jesus said, "Zacchaeus, today you became a child of mine because you have trusted me. I love you and will take care of you forever."

Lunch
Box

8 Acts of Disobedience

A Statue of Salt

(Genesis 19:12–17, 26)

God's Book tells us about people who didn't do what He had told them. They sinned just as you and I do when we don't obey our parents, teachers, ministers, policemen, or others who care for us. Not obeying is called disobedience.

There were two cities, Sodom and Gomorrah, which were very wicked. The people sinned so greatly that God decided to destroy them completely . . . their homes, stores, animals, and crops. Everything had to be burned! Fire would come down from heaven and destroy the cities.

But there was one man named Lot whom God didn't want to destroy. He was married and had two daughters living at home. So the Lord sent two heavenly visitors to see him and warn his family about the coming danger.

When the visitors arrived in the city they were teased and mocked. They stayed inside Lot's house because the sinful men of the city wanted to get them. God's messengers weren't even safe in these two towns!

In the morning God's men told Lot, "Take your wife and daughters and run for your lives. Go as far away as those mountains over there and don't turn to look back, not even once. God is going to burn these cities to the ground."

Lot quickly answered, "Gentlemen, I'm afraid to stay in the mountains. We may starve or wild animals may kill us. May we go instead to that little city?" He pointed to a small city at the foot of a large mountain.

God's messengers said, "All right. You may go to that city, but hurry! Go quickly!"

Lot, his wife, and daughters began running. And God began to burn the cities. He sent fire pell-melling out of heaven like hail. Everywhere and on everything sizzling fire bombed.

Lot and his family could hear the noises of burning as they ran. People screamed, homes went up in smoke, trees snapped, buildings crackled as they fell, dying cattle cried out. But Lot's family ran on because God had said not to look back.

Lot's wife thought about everything she left behind, her home, nice clothes, and the city she loved. All of it would soon be ashes and soot. These thoughts kept pestering her until she turned her head just a little to take one last, short peek at her hometown. Just as she did, God turned her into a solid statue of pure white salt!

Lot and his daughters could hear that she was no longer with them. She didn't answer their calls. Her footsteps were silent. "What happened to her?" they asked each other as they ran. No one knew and no one dared to turn and look because of God's command.

Trouble for Pharaoh

(Exodus 7:10–25; 8:5–32)

Moses and Aaron stood in front of King Pharaoh and announced, "Our God, the God of the Israelites, com-mands you to let  His people leave your land. You must let them go!"

But Pharaoh was stubborn. He shouted back, "I won't let them go." You see, the Israelites were his slaves. They did all the hard work in his kingdom. If he let all these people go, who would do the work? And so he said, "No!"

Because King Pharaoh disobeyed God, God told Moses to have Aaron stretch his walking stick over the waters of the kingdom. When he did this, every drop of water in every bowl, pond, lake, and river turned into red blood.

Fish can't swim and live in blood, you know. They turned over on their sides and died. Their bodies floated to the edge of the water and the beaches were soon covered with dead and rotting, stinking fish.

What happened when the people wanted to take a drink, take a bath, cook food, wash dishes, or water their gardens? Everywhere the water had turned to blood—right to the last drop.

For a long time the people of Pharaoh's kingdom were bothered by blood. Moses thought that Pharaoh would surely let the people leave now. And so he asked again. But Pharaoh shouted, "No! I will not, I will not!"

God told Moses to have Aaron stretch his stick over the river again. This time frogs came leaping and scrambling out. Not just a few came, but they kept coming out until frogs were everywhere; in the beds, cooking pots, dishes, food, washtubs, and the pockets of the people's clothes. Croaking and squiggling they came.

Acts of Disobedience

Pharaoh was so disturbed by them that he came to Moses saying, "Please, oh, please, take away these frogs and I will let the people go! If only we can get rid of all these frogs!"

God made all the frogs die. Now there were dead frogs everywhere. The people gathered them into huge piles . . . piles of stinking and spoiling frogs.

But when the frogs were gone, Pharaoh changed his mind. For punishment God had Aaron stretch his stick over the dust and tiny crawling lice appeared on all people and cattle. They lived in the hair of men and animals and bit their skin. People kept scratching their heads to get rid of the pests. They scratched until their heads were sore and bleeding, but the lice couldn't be killed.

Even that didn't make Pharaoh obey! So God sent swarms of flies to bother everyone, except the Israelites, God's people. This time only Pharaoh and his people were pestered. Flies buzzed in their ears and around their eyes. They landed on their noses and lips. The people almost went crazy trying to chase them away, but they couldn't get rid of them.

Pharaoh changed his mind again, but his heart was still just as hard as stone. He wouldn't let God's people leave after all of these awful plagues.

More Trouble
(Exodus 9, 10)

Then God sent a disease to all of the cattle of Pharaoh's land. It was a severe disease and all the cattle died: old and young, weak and strong, fat and thin. They fell over dead.

Still Pharaoh's heart was angry. His people begged and begged him to let the

Israelites go. They wanted to live in peace and pleasure again. But their stubborn King just wouldn't listen to their cries.

Next God sent boils to all the men and beasts. Boils are large red sores which are hard but terribly tender. These sores covered their whole bodies. They couldn't even lie down or sit without having great pain from the boils.

Another plague that God sent was hail, large round pieces of solid ice. Every garden and field was shredded to the ground. Their homes were shattered and pounded. Lightning flickered and thunder crashed.

Then God sent grasshoppers which covered the earth. They ate everything as they went. They mowed and shaved the earth. Finally only bare brown dirt could be seen across the land.

Darkness followed the grasshoppers. It was blacker than midnight for three days. The moon and stars didn't glitter, not even a little. People, animals, and pets stumbled through the days and nights. No one knew what time it was. They didn't know when to go to bed or get up. They bumped into things as they walked. Confusion was everywhere!

But Pharaoh still said, No! After all these dreadful things God sent to punish him, he still refused. God became angry with him. He planned to show Pharaoh that He meant what He said.

Trouble and Tears
(Exodus 12:21–36)

Moses told the Israelites about God's plan. He told them to pack and be ready to leave Pharaoh's land. He also told them to paint the top of their doors with the blood of a lamb. This would be a sign to keep them from receiving the next punishment God would send.

Night crept quietly into the kingdom. Israelites were preparing to leave, but Pharaoh and his people fell asleep easily, thinking that God had at last stopped bothering them. Yet that very night God sent an angel of death to every house except those that were painted with blood. The death angel gently touched the oldest child in every single home. Not a sound was made, but death had struck.

During the same night the king and his servants awoke. But in each house of Pharaoh's people, the oldest child didn't. Something was terribly wrong. Can you imagine how brokenhearted these people were when they realized what had happened?

Pharaoh, too, cried when he saw that his own precious child was no longer living. This touched and softened his hard, hard heart. At last he called for Moses, "Please, please, take the Israelites and

leave this land. Quickly
go before something
else happens to us!

When God gave
the command the
Israelites began to
move from Pharaoh's
land. Slowly they
inched out of the
country of slavery.
They were free at last! Joyfully the thousands of Israelites began their journey.

Dry Road Through the Sea
(Exodus 14:5–31)

Within a couple of days God's people
were stopped by the Red Sea. Moses asked
God to help them cross over. God helped
them that very night. He sent a strong
wind to push back the waters of the sea
until they stood up like cemented stone

walls. And the people began to walk across on the dry sea floor.

Two days also gave Pharaoh time to think. The longer he thought about losing all of his slaves, the more angry and impatient he became. When he could stand it no more, he called together his army and followed after the Israelites, hoping to catch them.

Pharaoh and his men caught up to them just as the last Israelites were walking across the dry sea floor. They hurried right into the sea after them. When the last Israelite climbed onto the shore, God hurled the walls of water back into the middle of the sea. Pharaoh and his men were covered with tons of water!

God punished Pharoah in a powerful way! What a sight! Pieces of chariots washed up on the beaches. Bits of broken wheels bobbed on the waves. Heavy weapons sunk to the bottom and began rusting. All of this was Pharaoh's punishment for disobedience!

Moses' Mistake

(Numbers 20:1–12)

Traveling through the desert was long and difficult. People complained to Moses about all the little things that they didn't like. One particular time they discovered that there was no water where they had camped. How disgusted they became. Whining and grumbling they came to Moses, "Whatever will we do now? There's not a drop of water near this place. The animals are thirsty and the children are hot and dusty. There's no water at all, not even for cooking. Things really cannot get much worse! If we have no water, we will surely die."

Moses cried to God, "See, Lord, how the people complain? They are really angry this time. Please help me give water to them."

God told Moses to go to a certain rock and speak to it. He promised that fresh water would gurgle and burst out of it. Then there would be water for everyone.

Moses listened to God. He too was worn from traveling. He was hot and his feet ached. He was tired of listening to the complaining Israelites.

When he walked to the rock, he was angry with them. Instead of speaking to the rock as God had told him, he furiously struck it with his cane, not once, but twice!

Water spurted out and hurried down the side of the rock.

The people grabbed pots and jugs. Quickly they filled them and scurried off to take care of their many chores. Now they were happy again, at least for a little while.

But God wasn't pleased, especially not with Moses. He had disobeyed. Instead of speaking to the rock, he hit it in a fit of temper.

Tenderly but firmly God spoke to Moses, "You have been a good leader of my people. You are bringing them nearer to the wonderful land I'm going to give them. But because you disobeyed, you'll not be allowed to go into that beautiful country. You may see it from a mountain-top, but you may not enter."

Moses was God's child and he loved God. But even God's children disobey. God had to punish Moses for this sin just as He will punish us for disobeying.

Man Overboard!

(Jonah 1, 2, 3:1–3)

God's voice visited Jonah one afternoon and gave him a command, "Go to Nineveh, Jonah! Preach the gospel to the people. They're so sinful. Tell them that their city will be overthrown if they don't ask for forgiveness." Quietly God slipped away, leaving Jonah alone to think about the command he had received.

But Jonah didn't want to preach. He ran away to a different city and got on a ship. He snuggled down into a corner and smiled and relaxed. He was so sure that he'd hidden from God.

How silly of him! Hide from God? It can't be done! God saw him sleeping peacefully in the ship. He sent a strong wind that stormed over the water. The boat slipped from tip to tip and edge to edge. Waves slammed against the sides like giant hammers. The captain called to the people to pray to their gods for safety. But Jonah slept on.

When the captain saw him napping, he shook him awake saying, "Get up, man! How can you sleep in a storm like this? Pray to your god for mercy!"

The other passengers were worried. They wondered whose fault this trouble could be. When they discovered that Jonah was the man, they begged, "Jonah, what shall we do? It is your fault that we are having this storm."

Jonah answered, "I guess you'll have to toss me overboard. Then the Lord will quiet the sea."

They did exactly that. Jonah was thrown over the side of the ship. Before he could drown, God sent a large sea creature to swallow him. Slowly he traveled down to its stomach. Can you think what it would be like to live inside the stomach of a fish? It must have been a whopper to take such a man-sized supper!

While Jonah lived inside this fish he prayed to God. He asked God to forgive him for disobeying and promised to go to Nineveh if God would save him and give him a second chance. Then Jonah waited as he rode inside this swimming fish.

Gliding through the water, the fish headed toward shore. Its stomach ached. Its supper wasn't as good as it seemed at first and this fish wanted to get rid of it fast. When it was as close to shore as a big

Acts of Disobedience

fish can come, it opened its gigantic mouth and vomited. Jonah was coughed out and he tumbled onto shore. He rinsed himself off and waded back to the sand.

The next time God asked him to go to Nineveh, he was ready to go and obeyed.

9 Deeds of Obedience

Pack Everything—We're Moving!
(Genesis 12:1–5; 13:14–18)

How do you think you would feel if God told you to move! Even if you knew exactly where you were going it would still be hard, wouldn't it? You'd have to leave your best friends, your favorite house and room, your school chums, and your church. Yes, you'd have to start all over in a new strange place.

That's just what God told Abram to do. He said, "Take everything you own and go to a new land. You don't even know where it is, but don't worry, for I will show you the way."

Abram and Sarai, his wife, began packing . . . dishes, furniture, tent houses, and clothes. Lot and his family did the same because they were going along. All of Abram's servants prepared to leave. Then there were Abram's many flocks and herds. They had to be gathered together. Picture in your mind what a long line that must have been!

If you were moving, you'd rent a truck or call a moving van. You could make a long journey in a few days. But all Abram had to use were wooden carts, horses, and donkeys. It took weeks and maybe even months!

Slowly the journey started. Animals clopped along. Saddles squeaked. Wagons and carts creaked as their wheels went round and round. Every night the noise quieted when the whole group stopped to camp and rest for the night.

Each day Abram started the journey again, wondering, "Where will God take me? What will the land be like? Will there be neighbors? I hope there's fresh water nearby. And I hope Sarai likes our new place!"

Each day they came closer to their new land. Each day Abram wondered if today would be the day they would arrive. He was anxious to see the new pastures and find the right spot to set up their home. It was like an exciting mystery.

Finally Abram and Lot separated. Their cattlemen were arguing and causing a lot of trouble. Lot and Abram decided that it would be best if they parted. Lot chose the land he wanted and headed in that direction with his family.

Then God called Abram and said, "Look to the south, north, east, and west of you. See the rolling land? I'm going to give you all of it, every inch you can see."

Abram stretched to take a closer look. He saw valleys and hills, pastures and fields. All of it, his! He was thankful to God for bringing him to this new home.

Bread for Tomorrow
1 Kings 17:8–17

Elijah was God's prophet. He spoke God's words to the people. And God took care of him. Sometimes God sent birds to bring him meat and bread. Elijah drank fresh, cool water from a brook. And when the brook dried up, the Lord sent him to another city. The Lord told him that a woman there would take care of him.

Elijah started out. He knew that somewhere in that city was a special person. God said so.

When Elijah walked into town, he saw a woman picking up sticks. She didn't look like she was very special. In fact, she looked like most other women. But Elijah was thirsty, so he spoke. "Hello, ma'am. Would you have time to get me a cup of water?"

"I'd be happy to," she said. "I'll be back in just a minute."

Elijah called out, "How about bringing me a slice of bread too?"

The woman's smile disappeared. She stopped and turned toward Elijah. "I'm so sorry. I can't give you a slice of bread. I don't have one. All I have is a little bit of flour. Not more than a cup. I have just a wee bit of oil. I was picking up sticks to build a fire. I thought I'd bake a little loaf of bread for me and my son. That's all I have. I'm so sorry."

"What will you do for food?" Elijah asked.

"I guess we'll starve." The woman looked so sad.

But Elijah knew God. He knew about God's plan. He knew about God's power. And so he said, "Don't worry about that. Go right in and bake your bread. Then give some to me. There will be enough left for you and your son."

The lady wondered, "But there is so little left."

Elijah knew that God wanted the woman to obey. "Go ahead. The Lord says that there will always be just enough left for you and your son."

The smile slowly came back to her face. "Okay. I will do as you say Elijah." Then she went into her house.

Quickly the woman built a fire. She mixed the flour and oil together and added a few other things. One small loaf was for Elijah. The other small loaf was for herself and her son. The bread smelled so good while it baked. It looked crusty and brown.

The woman peeked into her flour jar. She lifted the lid of the oil jar. And what do you think she saw? Elijah was right! There was enough flour and oil left for tomorrow.

Strange Weapons
(Judges 7:1–8, 15–23)

Gideon and his men were preparing for battle. Their enemy had many good soldiers. So Gideon called together every

man he could get and started getting them ready for war. But the Lord looked at Gideon's huge army and said, "Gideon, you have too many men. I want you to tell every man that is afraid to fight to go back home."

Gideon obeyed God. But when he announced this to his men, two out of every three of them left. That's way over half! Now Gideon's army was really quite small.

Again the Lord came to him and said, "Gideon, your army is still far too large. This time I want you to ask the men that are left to go to the water and get a drink. Then I will tell you who should go and who should stay to fight."

Obeying God again, Gideon sent his soldiers to get a drink. Most of them laid down their weapons and bent on their knees to get a drink. Drinking this way took quite a long time. But a few of them quickly bent over and lapped the water with their tongues, just as dogs drink.

Then God said, "Everyone that lapped up the water will stay to fight. All the other soldiers must leave."

Gideon watched closely. Out of every one hundred men, only three stayed! Gideon was left with only three hundred men to fight this important battle. If he wanted to disobey or was afraid to fight with so few men he could have simply forgotten God's command. But Gideon trusted the Lord and started off with three hundred men.

Before they came to the city they were going to fight, Gideon gave every man a trumpet, a pitcher, and a lamp inside each pitcher. Unusual weapons for battle, aren't they? He divided his men into three groups and quietly gave them their orders. Every man knew exactly what he should do and when he should do it.

The groups tiptoed around the city so that there was a group on each side of it. When Gideon gave the signal each man blew his trumpet and smashed his pitcher. Then they took the lamps out and blew the trumpets again. Finally they cried, "The sword of the Lord, and of Gideon."

The people inside the city jumped! What a terrible noise: trumpets blared; something was shattering and crashing and clanging. Suddenly they could see lights on all sides. The trumpets blasted again and then voices shouted, "The sword of the Lord, and of Gideon." It was like a dreadful nightmare!

Terrified by all of this, they ran. Every person in the city jolted up and raced out, hoping to get away safely. They imagined that thousands of soldiers surrounded their city.

Think of it! Only three hundred men with trumpets, lamps, and pitchers. Perhaps they were strange weapons for war, but using these was obeying God. And God gave them the victory.

10 Acts of Pride

The Death of a Rich Man

(Luke 16:19–31)

Jesus tells a story about a very rich and a very proud man. The rich man was both of these, rich and proud. He wore clothes of kingly purple made from fine linen and expen-

sive silk. Every day he ate very good food. He was able to buy anything he wanted.

Outside his door lay a poor hungry man. He was a sick man. Large open sores covered his body. Stray dogs hung around him and licked his wounds. He was thrilled if he could even get some of the crumbs or the garbage left from the rich man's meals.

When the rich man went out for a walk, he passed Lazarus, a starving beggar. He put his nose in the air and strutted past. He was too proud to feed him or help him get doctor's care.

One evening both the rich man and Lazarus died. Lazarus went to heaven to be comforted and healed. He lived with God Himself!

But the rich man did not go to heaven. When he had time to think, the rich proud man could understand why he was not allowed to go to heaven. He had been unfriendly and unloving to those he met on earth. He looked up to heaven and cried out in pain, "Please, help me! Come down and give me cool water to drink. I'm burning alive. I can't stand it."

One of God's saints answered back,

"When you were living, you wouldn't help Lazarus, not even once. You had plenty of money. You could have cared for him. But you thought you were too good. Now you are hurting and Lazarus is happy."

A Proud Man Prays
(Luke 18:9–14)

Jesus tells the story about two men who came to the Temple to pray. One was a Pharisee, a church leader. The other man was a publican. That means that he was a tax collector. When the Pharisee strutted up to pray he held his head high in the air. Proudly he looked toward heaven saying, "Dear Lord, I'm so glad that I'm not as bad as other people. They are cheaters, some have many women, and some are tax collectors who actually steal. I fast twice a week. I always give some of my money to the church. Thank you for helping me to be better than other men!"

While the Pharisee prayed, the publican was also talking to God. His hands were folded on his chest. He knew he was a sinner and he wanted God to forgive him. Praying, he asked, "God, be merciful to me. I am a great sinner. Please forgive me." His prayer was very short but he had humbly asked God for something he wanted, a clean heart.

Stop and think for a moment. Which man sounded really sorry for sinning? Did one of the men brag as if he was better than others? Which man stood with bowed head and folded hands?

God heard only one of these prayers. You know now which one it was. He heard the prayer of the tax collector. He knew he was a sinner. The Pharisee prayed as if he was perfect. Not once did he mention any of his sins. He thought he was too important to have to admit to his own wickedness. After all, he was a church leader! But his proud praying was ignored by God.

Who May Throw Stones?
(John 8:1–11)

One afternoon Jesus sat outside writing in the sand. He was thinking as he scribbled. But his thoughts were soon interrupted by a group of people who crowded around Him. They were pulling a woman into the group. They shoved her in front of Jesus and said, "See this woman! What a sinner she is. We caught her living with another man just as if she were married to him!"

They were talking fast because they were so excited. They had caught someone sinning and they had dragged her to Jesus. Finding fault with her was almost like fun. They even wanted to stone her to death!

Jesus completely ignored them. He acted like He was still alone. He continued writing in the sand and thinking.

But the crowd kept pushing the woman and calling, "Lord, don't you understand? This is a very wicked lady. She's done a terrible thing. Aren't you going to do anything to her or say anything at all?" They talked so proudly— just as if they were perfect and never had sinned at all.

The woman blushed, because she was embarrassed. The crowd was right. She had sinned and they had caught her living in another man's house. Nervously she waited, wondering what would happen to her.

Finally Jesus said to the crowd. "Any one of you that is perfect, has never done

one sin, may throw the first stone." Then He looked down again and continued writing in the sand. The crowd quieted down. Each one was looking into his own heart. They each saw a lot of very bad sins inside themselves. Jesus had said that only the perfect ones could throw stones. One by one they silently left. They were ashamed. How proud they had been to think they were so good. They had no right to pick on someone who was no worse than they were.

In a short time everyone had left. The woman stood alone with Jesus. He got up and said to her, "I will not stone you either. Go now, and sin no more."

11 Deeds of Humility

An Empty Pocketbook
(Mark 12:41–44)

Have you ever heard the word *humble?* Do you know what it means? It isn't hard to understand. It means the opposite of proud. A humble person doesn't brag and talk about how good he is or how much he can do. He does his good works quietly and sincerely.

There was a woman who was a widow, for her husband was dead. She lived alone and had very little money to live on. But she loved Jesus so much that she always saved out enough to bring to the Temple to help in the Lord's work.

One day she put on her better clothes and walked to the Temple. In her hand she held two mites. The coins were worth less than one penny in our money. You know that isn't very much, but it was all the money she had to bring.

When she came to the Temple, other people were dropping coins into the money box. One man was especially rich. His clothes were satin and velvet. He walked up to the box with a large bag of coins and poured in the whole bag of money. With a satisfied look he slowly walked away.

The widow knew that she had very little to give. She hurried up to the box, almost hoping no one would notice her. Quickly she dropped in her two small coins and hurried home. She wished that she had more to give.

Jesus saw both of these people, the rich and the poor. He told his friends that the widow had given far more than anyone.

Surprised, Jesus' friends said, "Wait a minute. How can that be? The poor widow dropped in two small coins. The rich man gave a whole bag full. Certainly the man gave more!"

"You're wrong," Jesus answered. "The rich man has many more money bags at home. He won't even miss the one he gave today. But the widow doesn't have even one penny left. She gave everything, every single penny she had. Indeed, she did give more!"

Father, Forgive Me!
(Luke 15:11–24)

With his money in his pocket and his clothes in a suitcase, a young man set out to live by himself. He left his older brother and father at home.

He wanted to live alone, so he could do exactly what he wanted to do.

He asked his father to divide the money that he and his brother would get someday. He took his half and proudly hurried off to see the world and have some fun!

In the first city he stopped, he rented an expensive apartment with fancy furniture. He hustled to the grocery store and bought bags of tasty but costly food. He invited people over to his house. He wanted friends and parties, lots of both!

Night after night he used his time and money this way. During the days he slept so he could feel wide awake for the night-time parties. "When did he work?" you ask. He didn't, and so his money was used up quite quickly.

When he had no money left, he went out to find a job. His friends left him. He wasn't any good to them now because he didn't have a cent. He couldn't rent the apartment and couldn't buy any food. He needed a job very badly.

But jobs were pretty hard to get. The country was having a bad year. The crops had not grown. There was little to eat. Few people could afford to hire another worker.

At last he had to be happy with the best job he could find—feeding pigs. He waded through the slop to throw corn to them. He slept in the fields near them. Every second he smelled their dirtiness. The pigs

stayed roly-poly on the dried corn, but he was starving. His stomach growled so long and loud that he almost wanted to eat pig's food.

While he sat in the mud and filth he thought to himself, "How stupid of me. I thought I was so smart to leave home. I wanted to be a big shot. Ha! Look at me ... feeding pigs. Some big shot I turned out to be! I wasted all my money and now I'm starving to death. Even my Dad's servants have more than I've got. Hmmm ... home ... dad .... good food — that's what I'll do. I'm going back to my father's house. I'll fall on my knees and beg his forgiveness."

As soon as he made the decision he jumped up and headed for home. His father noticed him coming in the distance and ran out to welcome him calling, "My son! My son! How happy I am to see you again!"

The runaway son fell on his knees and humbly asked his father to forgive him. Of course the happy father was thrilled to see him and forgave him immediately. His lost son was home at last!

12 Acts of Dishonesty

A Trick on Father
(Genesis 27:1–40)

Isaac was growing old and was going blind. He didn't know how much longer he'd live. So he called Esau, his older son, and said, "Go out and kill a deer. Bring the meat home and make me a bowl of stew, the tasty kind you make so well. Then I'll give you your blessing." Isaac wanted to do it soon because he was so old. He had no idea how long God would leave him on this earth.

Rebekah, Isaac's wife, heard Isaac talking to Esau. She wanted Jacob, the younger son, to get the blessing. Quickly she called Jacob in and told him, "Run out and kill two baby goats. I'll fix the spicy stew your father likes. Then you can give it to your father. You will have the blessing instead of Esau."

But Jacob wasn't so sure about this trick. He said, "But Mom, Dad will know the difference. Esau's arms are hairy and mine aren't. Besides he knows our voices. We sound different when we talk."

"Go and do what I've told you," Rebekah ordered him. "You must get the blessing. I will help you."

Jacob killed the baby goats and Rebekah made the stew. She put the goat skin on Jacob's arms and neck. Jacob put on some of Esau's clothes. Then he walked into his father's room, hoping the trick would work.

Isaac, hearing someone come into his room, asked, "Who is it?"

Jacob lied, "I am Esau, your older son. I am back with your stew. It's nice and hot and ready to eat, just the way you like it."

But Isaac suspected something. He said, "Come closer so I can touch you." He couldn't see the difference because his eyes were so weak and blurry. He hoped he could feel the difference.

When he touched Jacob's arms he said, "You sound like Jacob. But you feel like Esau." He rubbed his wrinkled, shaky hands over the skins. Then he added, "Are you really my son Esau?"

Jacob answered, "Yes, I am. I am."

Convinced at last, Isaac ate the stew and then raised his arms over Jacob to bless him. "You will be a rich man. You'll have all the food you can eat. You will be important. Many people will respect you and look up to you. God will stay with you always."

Jacob hurried off, happy that he had the blessing. He and his mother had to be dishonest to get it. Both of them stole the blessing from Esau, and Jacob also lied.

Seven Times Two

(Genesis 29:15–28)

Jacob hurried away from home because he was so afraid. Esau was furious with him for stealing his blessing. Esau even wanted to kill him. So Jacob rushed off to visit his Uncle Laban, who lived far away.

When he arrived at his uncle's house he was happy . . . happy to be away from Esau and happy with what he saw at Uncle Laban's. Laban had a daughter named Rachel. She was a very beautiful girl. Since Jacob was ready to marry, he naturally wanted Rachel for his wife. He fell deeply in love with her.

Jacob went to Laban and offered, "I will work for you for seven years if I may marry Rachel."

Laban agreed. Seven years of work would be a big help. And the work would be free! Jacob would be working to pay for or to buy Rachel for his wife.

Those years flew by because Jacob was eager to marry Rachel. He loved her so dearly. He thought how they'd set up their own house, get their own flocks, and have a family. In no time at all, those seven years were past.

The day of the wedding came. Can't you imagine Jacob's excitement? The bride walked in with a wedding veil that covered her face. That's the kind they wore in that country.

When the wedding was over Jacob and his new wife went home. When Jacob took off her veil he was shocked! He blinked his eyes. "Can it be true?" he asked himself. "Uncle Laban has given me Leah, Rachel's older sister! Oh, no!"

Jacob raced back to Laban and demanded, "I worked seven years to marry Rachel. But you've given me Leah. You tricked me. You've lied."

Of course Laban knew what he had done. He had been dishonest. He said,

"Jacob, in our country the oldest must marry first. Now that Leah is married you may marry Rachel if you wish. But you must work another seven years for her."

Jacob agreed to this because he loved Rachel so. He married Rachel, but he had to work another seven years. Altogether he worked fourteen years to marry the girl he loved.

Whose Baby?

(1 Kings 3:16–28)

Throughout the kingdom King Solomon was known for his wisdom. Whenever there was a difficult problem, people came to him. He was a great problem solver!

One day two women came into his throne room. They were screaming and arguing. They were fighting over something that one of the women was carrying. The King was quite surprised when he saw they were fighting over a baby!

"Quiet down, ladies," he said to them. "One at a time. Who would like to speak first?"

One of them began, "Last night we both went to bed with our babies. During the night she rolled over on hers and the baby died. Then she took my live baby and put the dead one by me."

Almost before she had finished talking the other woman started, "Oh, no! That's not how it happened at all! You rolled over on yours and gave me the dead baby. The live one is mine!"

In a moment they were fussing at each other again. King Solomon ordered them to be quiet for the second time. He wanted a little time to think. This wasn't an easy problem. A little baby is a very precious thing. He had to be certain to give it to the right mother. But how would he know? How would he know?

When he reached his decision he said, "Guards, bring a sword. We'll cut the baby in half so each of you may have half of it."

Everyone in the throne room looked surprised. Are you? Would Solomon really cut the baby in half? King Solomon was just testing the women. He wouldn't really do it. But the baby's true mother believed him. She was horrified! "Kill my baby," she cried, "never! Give him to the other lady. Then at least he will be alive!"

The mother of the dead baby didn't care. The live baby wasn't hers anyway. So she said, "That's a good idea. That'll be fair. We'll each have half."

Now King Solomon knew which was the real mother. She was the one that didn't want the baby to be hurt. He gave her the living baby and she hurried home to care for it.

Two Lies and Two Deaths
(Acts 5:1–11)

When Christ's church began hundreds of years ago, the people were very generous. They gave a lot of money to help each other, and they did it willingly.

Ananias and Sapphira, a married couple, owned some land. They sold it to be able to give more money to the church. But before they brought it they saved some of it out for themselves.

Ananias went to the church leaders first. He brought his wallet with him. When he took the money out and gave it to them, he said, "My wife and I sold some of our land. We're giving all the money to the church."

Peter, the church leader, knew he was lying. God had told him. Peter spoke to Ananias, "Why are you lying? You're obeying Satan. You have really saved part of the money for yourselves."

As soon as Peter said that, Ananias crumpled over in a heap on the floor. He died immediately. The church leaders took him outside and buried him.

About three hours later, Sapphira walked into the church. She was looking for her husband, Ananias. He'd been gone so long.

Peter saw her and asked, "Sapphira, did you and your husband sell some land? And are you giving all of the money to the church?"

"Yes," she quickly answered. She knew that she and her husband had agreed to lie about it. "My husband brought the money to you, didn't he?"

"You're right," Peter said. "But why did you and Ananias agree to lie? The same men who buried your husband will also bury you." No sooner had Peter spoken when Sapphira wilted to the floor, dead!

You may think that God was too strict with Ananias and Sapphira. After all, we don't have to give all of our money, do we? The answer is No. But their sin was lying. They should have told Peter that they sold their land and were bringing part of the money to the Lord. But they were dishonest.

Buried Treasure

(Joshua 7:10–11, 16–26)

There was only one command that the Lord gave His army before sending them to Jericho. He said, "Destroy the city completely. You may take gold and silver for the church treasury, but take nothing, absolutely nothing, for yourselves." The men left for battle and returned with the victory.

The next wicked city that had to be destroyed was Ai. Again the men went off to battle ready to fight and win. But they soon came running back. They had been beaten and chased away from the city of Ai.

Joshua, their leader, couldn't understand why the Lord had allowed them to be beaten. He called the Lord, "Why have you let us be chased? We're so ashamed. Everyone will call us losers. People will laugh at us."

God answered Joshua, "You lost the battle today because someone didn't obey

246   Acts of Dishonesty

my orders for the city of Jericho. Someone stole clothes and money from Jericho. Find him and burn him because he disobeyed. Then I will give you victories again."

Early in the morning, Joshua started the task. Finding the one man out of the thousands of Israelites would be a long and unpleasant job.

He called all the large groups together. There were twelve in all. As Joshua stood before each one the Lord said, "No, this is not the group of men that has the thief." But when Joshua stood in front of Judah's group the Lord said, "Yes, someone in this group has done it."

These groups were very large. There were a lot of families in each one. So Joshua had to call each family in front of him. One by one they came. For each one the Lord said No until Achan's family stood before Joshua. Then the Lord said, "This is the man."

Joshua told Achan, "Tell us what you've done."

Achan began his story, "When we were destroying the city of Jericho I saw so many things I wanted. There was a beautiful coat. I found five pounds of silver and more than a pound of gold. I couldn't resist them! So I took them. I hid them under my coat. When I got home I dug a hole under my tent and buried all of it."

Sure enough! The men that were sent to check his story found the coat, gold, and silver. It was buried exactly where Achan had said it would be. Achan was the thief.

God had a terrible punishment for him. Joshua was commanded to take Achan, his sons, his daughters, his oxen, his donkeys, his sheep, his tent, and everything Achan owned. He led them to a deep valley. God told the Israelites to destroy them completely. And they did. There was nothing left of Achan and his family and belongings but ashes. This was his punishment for stealing the clothes and the silver and gold.

A Stolen Wife

(2 Samuel 11:14–27; 12:15–18a)

David was a good king. His soldiers liked him and the people of his kingdom respected him. David was a man of God and God blessed him.

One evening David walked up to his palace roof to relax. The roof was flat and it was like a patio up there. While he was there he could look down upon the roofs of the houses around him. He happened to see a beautiful woman a couple of houses down. She was washing herself and cooling off. David saw her and wanted her.

He called to his servants to go and tell the woman to come to his palace. She came and she stayed with David, just as if she were his wife. But really she was married to another man.

Probably you're wondering, "Where was her real husband? Why did he let his wife obey the King and go to live with him?" Her husband couldn't say anything because he didn't know about it. He was away at war, fighting a battle for the King.

After they had lived together for a short while, the lady, Bathsheba, found out that she was going to have a baby. King David wanted to marry her because Bathsheba had been living with him. It was his baby too.

But how could he get rid of Bathsheba's real husband? He knew he couldn't marry Bathsheba as long as Uriah, her husband, was alive. He sat on his rooftop, thinking of what to do.

The next day he sent a message to his army commander. It read, "Put Uriah in the very front row of the battle where the fighting is fierce. These are orders from your King!"

Very soon King David got his wish. A note was delivered back to the palace door. It was from his army chief. David read the note to himself. It said, "King David, Uriah has been killed." The King not only stole another man's wife, but he also had her husband killed so he could marry her.

God was very unhappy with them. King David, His own child, had been dishonest. He had to be punished just as any other person. Soon after the baby was born it died. David wanted this baby to live so badly. But God took it away from him because of his sin.

13 Sins of Idolatry

Worshiping a Calf

(Exodus 32:1–6, 19–29)

Do you know if you have ever seen an idol? Do you know what is meant by an idol? It is anything you worship or the thing that you love most of all. Clothes and money are idols for some people. It is all they can think about. Others use new cars as idols. Some have little figures or statues that they worship instead of God. Christians may not have idols. We are to worship God and love Him above everything else.

While Moses was leading the Israelites out of Egypt, the people fell into the sin of idolatry. God had called Moses up to a mountaintop so He could talk with him. Moses was with God for a very long time.

The Israelites thought that Moses wasn't coming back.

They came crying to Aaron, "Moses is surely gone for good. He'll never come back. We need something to worship! Aaron, will you please make us some gods?"

Aaron really knew better. He knew that it is sinful to worship statues or idols. But instead he said, "Bring all of your earrings to me . . . all the nice golden dangling ones that your wives and your children wear. I will make you a beautiful golden statue for your worship. It will be your god who brought you out of the land of Egypt."

The people scattered quickly. They went from tent to tent collecting earrings. They filled baskets full of them. When the last earring was gathered they brought the collection to Aaron.

Carefully he melted the jewelry over a hot fire. Then he shaped it into the figure of an animal. He carved and chiseled until it looked exactly like a calf... a golden calf! He polished it until it glittered in the sun. Then he placed it in front of the people.

As soon as they saw their glistening idol, their new god, they liked it. They made sacrifices and bowed low before their golden god. Imagine! People praying to a chunk of gold as if it could hear them! How silly and sinful these grown-ups were acting!

God could see what His people were doing. He was angry with them. It seemed to Him that they would never learn—that they would never really turn away from sinning.

Moses saw it too. He hurried down the steep slopes. In his hands he held two tablets of stone. God Himself had written the Ten Commandments on these heavy tablets. As Moses came closer and closer to the bottom of the mountain, the

more disgusted he became. Finally he flung the stone tablets in anger. They lay on the ground in bits and pieces.

Later Moses burned the golden calf until it melted. And when it was cool, he ground it into a fine powder. Slowly he sprinkled it over the water and made the people drink it.

I don't know what the ashes of burnt gold would taste like. But I can imagine that they must have choked and gagged on it. Later three thousand people who had worshiped the idol were punished. God's own people should have known better than to worship an idol!

A Contest

(1 Kings 18:17–40)

Baal was worshiped by some of the people in King Ahab's country. They built altars to this god and made statues of him. But others honored God, the only true Lord. And so it went—the people kept arguing about who was truly God Himself. Some worshiped the true God; others didn't.

In this land there was a prophet of God named Elijah. He wanted to show the people that God alone should be loved, that

He is the only true God. Elijah asked King Ahab to send the prophets of Baal to Mount Carmel. He had something special in mind.

There were four hundred and fifty prophets of Baal that came. Elijah was the only prophet of God. Together they climbed this mountain while the people followed closely behind.

When all the prophets and people reached the top of Mount Carmel Elijah announced, "Today we're going to find out which god is truly God. Men, bring two little bulls for the sacrifice. You prophets of Baal, build an altar to Baal. I'll build one for my God. Then we'll both ask our gods to send fire from heaven to burn our sacrifices. Whichever god does that will be named God of all."

The prophets of Baal agreed. They built their altar, put the sacrifice on top, and called to Baal. "Oh, Baal, hear us! Send fire to show that you are God."

While they called they kept dancing. They thought that their god would surely hear and see them.

All morning this continued. They sang and danced and called to Baal. But Baal wasn't answering them. Elijah began to tease them a little, "Maybe Baal is on his vacation. Or he may be napping. Perhaps if you will call a little louder, he just might wake up."

The prophets of Baal were getting very worried about their god. Where could he be? They cried louder. They danced faster. They shouted and screamed. Oh, how badly they wanted Baal to answer them.

When evening finally came, there was no fire to burn Baal's sacrifice. He had not heard them. He hadn't answered them because Baal was only an idol. He was not God at all.

Then Elijah called the people around him. He built an altar from twelve stones.

He put a ditch around it. He cut the little bull in pieces and put them on the altar. Then he poured many buckets of water over the altar until it was soaked and the ditch was full.

The people watched him, wondering, "Why did he soak the altar? Doesn't he know that anything wet will not burn? How can any god burn a dripping wet altar?"

Elijah stood before the people and prayed to God, "Dear Lord, let the people know that you are the only true God. Send fire from heaven to burn this sacrifice. Then they will worship you as the only true God."

Silently everyone waited. They wondered if they would have to wait another whole day as they did for Baal. Elijah wasn't dancing around. He wasn't shouting. He stood prayerfully and trusted the Lord to answer him.

Before the people realized what had happened, fire shot from heaven like falling stars. It snapped and crackled as it ate up the meat and drank the water. Yes, even that sopping wet altar was licked until it was black and dry!

The people were amazed. They were shocked. They fell down on their knees and worshiped God. They knew for certain that Baal wasn't God. At last they knew and believed the true God. The prophets of Baal were captured and punished for their idolatry.

Living for Money

(Luke 18:18–23)

A young ruler came to Jesus and asked, "Good teacher, what do I have to do to go to heaven when I die?"

Jesus answered, "You must obey all the commandments. Be careful not to kill. Never steal or tell a lie. And always be kind to your mom and dad."

A smile flashed across his face when he heard that. He spoke quickly, "I've done all of that. I do keep the commandments. I'm very careful about that. I have kept all the commandments ever since I was a boy."

"But there's one more thing," Jesus added. "You must sell all your belongings and give your money, all of it, to the poor people. Then you will go to heaven."

The smile dropped from his face as thoughts galloped through his mind. "Give away all my things?" he asked himself. "I can't do it. I'm too rich. If I did that I'd be a beggar. I could never give away all my clothes or sell my brand-new house. Besides I've saved a lot of money. I couldn't stand to give it away." Without saying any more to Jesus he turned and trudged toward home. He wasn't willing to do that for heaven!

Why did Jesus tell him to give away everything he had? Jesus didn't say that because all God's people must do it in order to go to heaven. He said it because He knew this rich man loved his money; it was his idol. It meant more to him than going to heaven. The rich man kept his idols but he missed the glory of living forever with God!

14 Jesus Is Coming Again

Watching for Jesus

(Matthew 24:36–42; Acts 1:11)

You have read stories about many kinds of sins. You have also read about people who pleased God. If you are one of God's children, you will always try to obey Him. You will look for that day when Jesus will come again. Won't that be marvelous! Every dead person will be raised from his or her grave. Every living person, every one of them, will watch Jesus floating down from the clouds. This is the very important day all Christians are waiting for.

But what should we do until then? The Bible tells us to watch for Him. What does that mean? Should you stop playing with your friends or quit going to school?

Should your dad quit his job? Should your family go to the top of a mountain and watch the sky for this exciting day? Just what does the Bible mean when it tells us to watch?

God wants us to watch with our hearts, not our eyes. He certainly doesn't want us to twiddle our thumbs and watch the clouds, because no one knows when that day will be. It would be wasting our time to sit and wait. He wants us to be anxious for that day. He wants us to hope for it. It should be the day that we're most eager for . . . more excited for it than for our next birthday or Christmas or anything at all. Jesus wants us to have our hearts ready to greet Him.

Learning About Jesus
(2 Timothy 2:15)

Is it enough to have our hearts ready for Him? No, we must do more. We must read the Bible, God's Book. It tells us how we should live. It answers our questions about what we should do.

"Oh, dear," you're thinking. "I can't read the Bible. It's too hard. Sometimes I don't even understand it. There are so many big words in it."

There's something you can do instead, at least until you're old enough to read it yourself. You should listen carefully when someone does read the Bible. Listen and try to understand. Some of the stories you'll know. Listen for new things. Listen to them on the radio or on records, and in Sunday

school. Maybe you can't use your eyes to read, but you can use your ears to listen.

There's one more thing God tells us about reading or listening to the Bible. We must believe it. God is telling us very special things that He wrote for us to hear. We must never think, "Oh, that couldn't be true." God wrote the whole Bible. He would never write a lie. It is all truth and we must believe it.

Talking with Jesus
(Matthew 6:5–6; Mark 11:24–25)

We must also pray to Jesus. Praying is talking to God and listening carefully in your heart for Him to talk to you.

Just what should you talk about when

you do talk to Him? Tell Him exactly what is on your mind. When you're happy, tell Him and tell Him why. He likes us to be happy people. If you're sad, tell Him and tell Him why. Ask Him for help. If you've been naughty, ask Him to take that sin away. Thank Him for all the good things He gives you.

You probably want to know if you should ask Him for things. The answer is Yes. If you really need something, ask

Him for it. Maybe you want a dog or a new tricycle or a two-wheeler. Should you ask Him for it? You don't really need it, but you'd like to have it.

Certainly you may ask for these things. But always remember that there are two answers, Yes and No. If God answers Yes, thank Him for giving it to you. If He answers No, thank Him for hearing your prayer, even though He answered No. Remember God always does what is best for you.

Where should you pray? When should you pray? You may pray in any place and at any time . . . on the playground, in your bedroom, before you eat, while you're doing the dishes, or any other time. Usually we fold our hands and close our eyes to show God that we honor Him. In your bedroom you might pray on your knees. But if you want to talk to Jesus at other times, just close your eyes a minute and whisper a little message to Him. If you believe on Him, He will hear all your prayers. Always remember to pray!

Living for Jesus

(Matthew 5:43–48)

Jesus also wants us to be very busy working for Him. He also wants us to show our love to others. If we really have this love in our hearts we can show it in so many ways!

One way is by being happy. Smile around the house. Whistle or sing a little tune. But be very careful about that grumbling! That is Satan's work. Whenever you're tempted to say bad things, don't!

Push Satan out of your heart. Ask God to help you.

If one of your friends is sick, make him a get well card. Take it over to his house or send it through the mail.

Visit Grandma and Grandpa if you have them. They love to see their grandchildren. Cheer them up by coming into the house with a big smile on your face.

Be careful when you're playing. Be kind to your friends. God wants you to

take turns. Share your things. Never cry and shout just because you didn't get what you wanted. God doesn't want his little Christians to be stingy.

Help your mom and dad. Sometimes they're so busy and get pretty tired. Put on a smile and offer to help clean the garage or help put the clothes away.

Be careful how you speak. Always do it quietly and kindly. Don't scream and holler. It's so much more pleasant to hear people speaking softly, isn't it? If you are careful not to shout when you speak

to others, they will be careful not to holler at you.

Can you think of more ways to show love and kindness?

Telling About Jesus
(Mark 16:15–16)

There's one more thing. You must tell other children about Jesus and how He loves little children.

Tell the little boy or girl that lives next door or down the street a little ways. If a child doesn't go to Sunday school he or she doesn't know our Jesus. Or better yet, take your friend along with you when you go. Maybe you have a Bible story book or a record you could lend. Then he or she can listen to these stories at home too.

Always be ready to talk about Jesus. If we love Him as much as we say we do, then we'll just have to tell others. This is

a very important part of being a Christian boy or girl or mother or father.

Now stop and think of all the things you and I must do until Jesus comes again ... watch for Him with our hearts, read the Bible, pray, show kindness to others, and tell the good news about Jesus. That's quite a list, isn't it? It will keep us very busy if we are really doing all of these things for our Lord. Isn't it wonderful to believe in Jesus!